Dale's Tale

HELEN JAYNE

BAAF
ADOPTION
& FOSTERING

Published by
British Association for Adoption & Fostering
(BAAF)
Saffron House
6–10 Kirby Street
London EC1N 8TS
www.baaf.org.uk

Charity registration 275689 (England & Wales)
and SC039337 (Scotland)

British Library Cataloguing in Publication Data
A catalogue record for this book is available from
the British Library

ISBN 978 1 905664 91 7

Project management by Shaila Shah, Director of Publications, BAAF
Cover design by Helen Joubert
Designed by Andrew Haig & Associates
Typeset by Fravashi Aga
Printed in Great Britain by T J International
Trade distribution by Turnaround Publisher Services, Unit 3,
Olympia Trading Estate, Coburg Road, London N22 6TZ

BAAF is the leading UK-wide membership organisation for all
those concerned with adoption, fostering and child care issues.

The paper used for the text pages of this book is FSC certified.
FSC (The Forest Stewardship Council) is an international network
to promote responsible management of the world's forests.

Printed on totally chlorine-free paper.

FSC
Mixed Sources
Product group from well-managed
forests and other controlled sources

Cert no. SGS-COC-2482
www.fsc.org
© 1996 Forest Stewardship Council

Contents

Acknowledgements

The very moment I thought about adopting Dale, to the actual publication of this story, has proved to be an emotional journey for many involved. It is with this in mind that I want to thank my wonderful family for standing by me during the turbulent times. In particular, David for "not saying no", Jordan for her many words of wisdom and countless cups of tea, Mum and Dad for their help and advice and, of course, Cate and Dale for being so adorable. I love you all very much.

Additionally, I want to thank BAAF for publishing my story and Hedi Argent, my enduring editor, for her help and total patience as well as her unshakeable belief that "we will get there in the end".

About the author

I have lived in an old mining community in Wales since 1998, but was born in another area famous for its coal – the Rhondda Valley. I have an honours degree in English and am director of a company that I run together with my husband. I married David in 2002. We had our younger daughter together and began fostering that same year; we have shared our home with a variety of children, from babies to teenagers. In June 2006, my husband and I adopted Dale, the little boy we had been fostering for two years. Now, both younger children are attending school and my eldest daughter has recently graduated with an English degree. Like me, she has a passion for writing and plans to take up a journalism course later this year.

I hope *Dale's Tale* is the first of many books I write. It has been an interesting experience but one that I would not have missed for the world.

For Dale

who made this book possible

The Our Story series
This book is part of BAAF's Our Story series, which explores adoption experiences as told by adoptive parents.

Also available in the series:
• *An Adoption Diary* by Maria James
• *Flying Solo* by Julia Wise
• *In Black and White* by Nathalie Seymour
• *Adoption Undone* by Karen Carr
• *A Family Business* by Robert Marsden
• *Together in Time* by Ruth and Ed Royce
• *Take Two* by Laurel Ashton
• *Holding on and Hanging in* by Lorna Miles

The series editor
Hedi Argent is an independent family placement consultant, trainer and freelance writer. She is the author of *Find me a Family* (Souvenir Press, 1984), *Whatever Happened to Adam?* (BAAF, 1998), *Related by Adoption* (BAAF, 2004), *One of the Family* (BAAF, 2005), *Ten Top Tips for Placing Children in Families* (BAAF, 2006), *Josh and Jaz have Three Mums* (BAAF, 2007), *Ten Top Tips for Placing Siblings* (BAAF, 2008), and *Ten Top Tips for Supporting Kinship Placements* (BAAF, 2009). She is the co-author of *Taking Extra Care* (BAAF, 1997, with Ailee Kerrane) and *Dealing with Disruption* (BAAF, 2006, with Jeffrey Coleman), and the editor of *Keeping the Doors Open* (BAAF, 1988), *See You Soon* (BAAF, 1995), *Staying Connected* (BAAF, 2002), and *Models of Adoption Support* (BAAF, 2003). She has also written five illustrated booklets in the children's series published by BAAF: *What Happens in Court?* (2003, with Mary Lane), *What is Contact?* (2004), *What is a Disability?* (2004), *Life Story Work* (2005, with Shaila Shah) and *What is Kinship Care?* (2007).

Foreword

When BAAF's Director of Publications first asked me to review a copy of this book about a foster carer who goes on to adopt her foster child against the wishes of the child's local authority, I thought...Oh no, not another swipe at my colleagues!

As someone who has been a social worker and a manager in fostering and adoption since the mid-seventies, I know that some of the most successful plans for children have acknowledged that the best place for them is to stay where they are...with their foster carers. This means nearly all the uncertainty is removed because both child and carers know each other and the placement is pretty much "tried and tested".

But I also know that often social workers have anxieties about children staying permanently with their "short-term" foster carers: they might feel the carer cannot fully meet the child's needs over the longer term, or they might worry that another "good", experienced foster carer is lost because this placement will take them off the books, at least for the immediate future. This said, no social worker should oppose such an adoption plan if it would be the best outcome for the child concerned.

Fostering agencies, be they in the voluntary sector or

the public sector, invest much energy and resource in recruiting and training foster carers. They begin to reap the rewards of their investment as they manage to place a range of children over a period of time. Children like Dale, who tempt foster carers away into adoption, frustrate the agencies' plans, albeit for the very best of reasons! We know that adoption is a successful outcome for 80 per cent of children placed, and transforms children's lives by attaching them to a permanent family for life.

I settled down to read the book anticipating what the story would be. But the first thing I want to tell you about it is that I read it in one sitting, eager to find out what happened next!

The arrival of this young baby, Dale, into the foster carer's home, and her angst about accepting him following the pain that she and the rest of her family had experienced when they "helped to move on" another young child for adoption, all contribute to setting the scene for this emotional journey. Helen tells us of her family members' reaction to Dale's arrival and how he won them all over.

This book is a story about the power of attachment and how it fuelled the foster carer's struggle against her supervising social worker and the managers in the child's local authority to win through and adopt Dale. Helen found some unexpected allies along the way, who sustained her in her darker moments. Unusually, Helen and her husband had only recently had their own child – just a few months before Dale was placed – and I am sure this would have concerned the local authority.

However, this is Helen and Dale's story and is told from the foster mother's perspective. I hope you enjoy it as much as I did; I believe you will be left in no doubt about how children can steal away your heart.

Mo O'Reilly
Director of Child Placement, BAAF

1

How it all began

It's kind of funny how your life can change direction in almost an instant. When I was in my early thirties I totally believed that I would remain a divorced mother of one, with a fairly worthwhile career, most likely in the health service, with little or no money worries and no real desire to embark on another serious relationship. When I met David in 1996, it was immediately clear that he had no interest in a casual relationship whatsoever. From the start, he was keen to settle down and play happy families and I surprised myself by feeling an urge to do the same thing.

When David and I married in 2001, we were quite content that my thirteen-year-old daughter, Jordan, might well be the only child we would raise together. We talked a bit about having another child and agreed that if it happened, we would both be delighted, but neither of us felt that we really needed to have a baby of our own in order to cement our relationship. Never in a million years did we, at that point, contemplate adoption. Yet here we are, thirteen years into our relationship, with Jordan just turned twenty-two, Cate aged seven, a beautiful "made together" daughter, many foster children who have come and gone, and a small bundle of mischief aged five, named Dale, whom we adopted in June 2006.

Our house, which seemed enormous when we purchased it in 1998, is now bursting at the seams with all sorts of paraphernalia, consisting of too much junk, assorted paperwork, which never seems to get filed, ironing, which I am certain belongs to at least five different families, and most of all, toys, toys and more toys. I like to think it is a happy if slightly humdrum family home, although sometimes, when I'm in the middle of ironing school uniforms, and pouring milk shakes whilst re-attaching Thomas the Tank engine's wheels or Barbie's head, I do question the sanity of some of the choices we have made. I'm pretty certain that various neighbours wonder somewhat at what goes on in the house, especially when our two youngest children can be heard screaming shrilly or crying bitterly during one of the many fights following a minor disagreement about who is the biggest or who broke the TV control again.

On occasions, I still ask myself how this all came about. What actually happened to the well-laid plans I thought I had made for mine and Jordan's future? The reality is that David and I never had a deep meaningful conversation or discussed in any great detail the chances of me getting pregnant. However, we did have many a discussion about adoption once Cate was born.

About three years before David and I married, we bought a beautiful home on the side of a mountain in an old mining community. This house had four bedrooms, which rapidly evolved into the master suite, that David and I commandeered, much to Jordan's disgust, Jordan's spacious room over the garage – to give us protection from her desire to play her stereo at top volume – another room that became a guestroom, and the fourth, which we turned into a study. At the time, this was probably the most well-used room in the house: David did all his paperwork there, and as a "wanabee" author, I could regularly be found tapping away at the word processor, whilst Jordan, an avid student, always used the room to do her homework. Downstairs, the house was colossal compared to our previous home. We were now the proud owners of a huge kitchen, a massive lounge, a separate dining room and another sitting room. It seemed like we would never be able to use all that space. Our dog, Fudge, loved the new house too. Never a great one for the outdoors, she could walk for hours around this place and get plenty of exercise. On top of that, there was a field-like garden in which you could quite easily lose yourself and half the street if you felt the urge to do so. It was actually during a conversation about how big the house was that the subject of fostering first came up. I had seen an advert for foster carers in the local press and I was interested because I was rather discontented with my job as a clerical officer at a local hospital, and felt I needed a change. I asked David how he would feel about us offering a temporary home to other people's children. We discussed it in some depth and David's broad view was that he would not object to giving it a go if I felt it would be something I would enjoy. We agreed that our home was spacious enough; in fact, it was crying out for more children.

At that point we filled Jordan in on our plans and suffered a bit of a setback; she was dead set against our inclination to become foster carers. She had been an only child for thirteen years and did not relish the prospect of change. I could understand her point of view, but I believed it would be a good thing for all of us if we were able to help another child by opening up our home. I tried hard to convince her. It was not easy. We had intense conversations about what it would be like living with someone else's child, and, although Jordan is a very compassionate person, it took weeks and weeks of gentle persuasion before she would even consider the idea of becoming a foster family.

When I eventually contacted some agencies and received literature about fostering, Jordan was still not totally on board, and I had concerns that she might never accept our decision. Finally though, she came around sufficiently for me to telephone a local independent fostering agency and arrange to meet with a very amenable sounding social worker by the name of Dan Lewis.

When I was starting this book, I called my eldest daughter and asked her to cast her mind back and tell me how she had really felt about the prospect of us fostering.

'Well, I'd love to say that I was absolutely delighted and eagerly anticipating sharing the house with other people's kids, but... in truth, I was apprehensive, jealous and, if I'm digging deep, quite crestfallen actually!'

At the time though, I honestly thought we had all come to a family decision and on a cold day in February 2000, Dan knocked at the door. I had made arrangements to meet him on my own, as Jordan was at school and David was in the middle of a stock check at work and unable to take any time off. Dan and I sat down to a steaming cup of tea and chatted about lots of things in general and then about fostering in particular. Straight away I found myself liking this social worker, who was friendly and funny and certainly put me at my ease. I recently asked him what his first impression was of me. He replied, and I quote, *'I instantly thought you were a very warm and friendly person. I felt comfortable with you immediately and thought you were completely open and honest about your reasons for wanting to foster. It was also very clear that your life had not been totally rosy and that you had experienced plenty of ups and downs, including divorce and bringing a child up on your own. Also, when I'm about to start an assessment of prospective foster carers I always ask myself, "Would I leave my own children with these people?" With you I felt the answer was definitely 'yes.'*

After the initial meeting with Dan, which I felt

extremely positive about, I spoke again with David and Jordan and we agreed to take things further and begin the assessment. This took a number of months, and even got put on hold for a time while David and I planned our wedding in the Dominican Republic in August 2001. When we returned, we went on with the assessment and eventually, in November 2001, Dan called us to say there was only one more meeting to go before our application went to the fostering panel for approval. What he didn't know was that I also had some big news for him.

It was rather a nerve-wracking experience, sitting in the kitchen opposite Dan knowing what we were about to tell him. David took a deep breath and said, 'Well Dan, there is no easy way to say this. Helen is pregnant!'

Dan's response was totally unexpected. 'Thank God!' he said. 'I thought for a minute that you guys had changed your mind about fostering.'

I started laughing, and so did David, but I really don't think Dan quite knew what to do. In the event, we all decided to take the weekend to think about what the next move should be.

That left the problem of Jordan. I believed that as we had, very prematurely, told Dan about the forthcoming baby, it was only right to let Jordan know at the earliest moment. She came in from school and I made her a cup of tea, then took a deep breath and asked gently:

'Jordan, how do you feel about having a baby brother or sister?'

Her answer was a bit of a shock.

'Oh my God! How can you do this to me Mum?' Swiftly and even more hurtfully:

'My friends must think you are at least forty!'

Cheers Jordan!

It took a lot of cuddling and a pair of designer trainers to even get Jordan to talk about what it would be like to have a new brother or sister. David and I also spent a lot of time trying to decide how best to move forward, and after some intense discussion we agreed that even though I was pregnant, nothing had fundamentally changed regarding our plans to foster. We were exactly the same people that we had been before the pregnancy, so we would go ahead and finalise our fostering assessment and then leave it to the panel to decide whether or not to place children in our care. Jordan remained unconvinced about the whole thing; when we tried to engage her in conversation, she would glare darkly at us and mutter under her breath. What on earth had happened to the sunny child I once had?

In early January 2002, we attended the panel meeting in Bristol. Surprisingly, Jordan agreed to come with us – although I did wonder whether she would leap to her feet at the very last minute and shout out a loud resounding *'NO!!!'*

Of course, she didn't. She was totally supportive and very articulate when panel members asked her opinion. She came across as well balanced, secure and fairly content with our choices. She did, however, ask if it would be OK to have a lock on her bedroom door to guard her privacy. That question made them smile. The Chair even told her how sensible she was and assured her it would be perfectly acceptable to get a lock put on her bedroom door. I didn't have the heart to enlighten them: Jordan was, in truth, more concerned about her impending sibling creeping unobtrusively into her room than about a foster child doing a similar thing.

That day, the panel approved us without reservations, for one child or two siblings aged 0–18 years. David and I were delighted. Jordan was resigned. Three weeks after their decision, our fostering agency called us to put us on alert for an imminent placement. A young woman, known to social services, had been admitted to hospital and was about to give birth; the child was to be removed from her care almost immediately. Indeed, three days later we were notified that a three-day-old baby boy was to be placed with us. It was an exhilarating moment, both scary and exciting. Even Jordan, for all her indifference, was grudgingly anticipating the huge change to all our lives. I particularly remember the evening before the new baby was due to arrive; we were in the car trying to remember all the nursery rhymes we knew so we could sing to him. Our fostering journey was about to begin.

* * *

When we decided that fostering was indeed something we would like to do, we examined the various organisations and options available to us. As I was intending to give up paid employment to foster, we decided that becoming part of an independent fostering agency instead of fostering for the local authority was probably our best option. The monetary rewards at that time were far greater if you were a carer for an independent organisation and in order to keep our large home running, money was an important factor. In addition, after speaking to a number of people who worked for Dan's agency, I felt that I would get plenty of emotional support from them – more than I could expect from our local authority. I thought this was very important as I was certain I would need lots of advice and help, particularly at this early stage. The downside of the choice we made was that it was often the more difficult children who were placed by the independent agencies, whilst social services placed more "run of the mill" children with their own foster carers. I understood that only if the local authority had no carers available, would they commission private organisations. The authority would then agree a payment, which would include the foster carer's reward, clothing and holiday allowances for the child, Christmas and birthday bonuses as well as a sum to the agency itself as the "middle man".

As a foster carer working for an independent agency, I could expect fortnightly visits from my own supervising support worker, a qualified social worker affiliated to the agency; various visits, some unscheduled, from the child's local authority social worker; a number of "Looked After Children" reviews or meetings, which included all parties involved in the care of the child; and training sessions and courses, such as health and safety and first aid. I was further expected to attend a support group on a monthly basis. Life changed overnight.

The months that followed were often very demanding and sometimes frantic. My pregnancy progressed well and looking after Timothy was a delight. He was a beautiful baby – happy and good tempered. He remained with us for almost a full year and he was about to turn one when, with bittersweet feelings, we met the people who had been chosen to adopt him. After an initial introduction, social services made arrangements for a gradual transition to allow Timothy to get to know his new parents-to-be. For a week we alternated between taking Timothy to his new home and his new parents visiting ours. We made every effort to remain in high spirits and positive for Timothy, as we did not want him to sense our sadness but it was a very difficult time as we knew that he would soon be gone. Timothy though, seemed to adjust to the new situation very well. He quickly took to his new mum and dad and it was clear that he would be loved and cherished by them. That in itself made me glad for him. However, the day I actually said goodbye, it was one of the hardest things I have ever had to do. On the morning, I carried him from his cot for the last time and cuddled him as long as I could before his social worker arrived to drive him to his new home and the start of his new life. It was a truly hard day not just for David, Jordan and me, but also for our extended families who had also treasured our first foster child. For a time, I couldn't bring myself to accept another placement as I couldn't imagine another child in the room that had been Timothy's. Ultimately though, other children needed us and I tried to move on.

Our very own little bundle of joy, Cate, was already five-and-a-half months old when Timothy left. Where had the time gone? It was, of course, hard for us all to adjust to life without Timothy but I, in particular, did not handle the transition very well. With hindsight, I realise that I must have been extremely difficult to live with – constantly weepy and depressed. I badly missed our little Timothy and so did Jordan. I felt desperately sorry for her during this period, as she had clearly bonded with Timothy and was now grieving. I felt consumed with guilt. Jordan had been against us fostering; we had somehow pushed her into it and now the feelings of loss and unhappiness were affecting her. In my own emotional state, I was ill equipped to help her come to terms with the situation. We spent long hours in tears together, talking about Timothy. I really feel that Jordan helped me at this time much more than I helped her. I also believe there was an added complication: I think I was suffering from some form of post-natal depression. My life had been so hectic since Cate's birth; looking after two small babies separated by only five months was challenging. I was certainly deprived of sleep. On reflection, it is obvious to me that I should have sought some help, possibly family counselling, and maybe things would have got easier sooner, but at the time I just kept hoping time would heal, and Jordan and I would eventually feel better.

I did, however, speak candidly with the foster agency we worked for. I requested that no more babies be placed with us unless they came as a mother and baby placement; if the baby already had a main carer, I wouldn't bond with it in the same way. Luckily the agency readily agreed. It took a long time for me to recover, but in due course the healing process did kick in, and with the arrival of new foster children, my days were once more taken up by routines and nurturing various youngsters with different needs and difficulties. Jordan, too, seemed to get over the shock of losing Timothy. And of course life went on. Not the same as before, but equally as exciting and challenging. And so the months rolled by.

2

Fostering Dale

July 28th 2004 started in much the same way as any other day. The thing that made it rather special for me was that it was my youngest brother Adam's 23rd birthday – and that was really worth celebrating. Only a year before he had plunged from a third-storey window, sustaining dangerous head injuries from which he was extremely lucky to recover. That accident had been a pivotal point in my life, as for the first time I had to come to terms with the prospect of the death of a loved one. The horror of seeing Adam lying heavily sedated in the intensive care unit, his brain dangerously swollen, his body cut and bruised, was a stark warning to us that life is fragile and too fleeting to be wasted. On the day we knew he would get better, I vowed that I would change the way I lived, and grasp opportunities that came my way with passion and enthusiasm instead of, as was my usual manner, being prudent and turning my back on whatever did not look a totally safe bet. And so, at 9am on that beautiful summer's day, my mind was on how Adam was going to spend his day on the Costa del Sol, where he and his girlfriend had recently moved to run a bar.

David and I had now been fostering for two-and-a-half years, Jordan was already sixteen and Cate had turned two. During this time, we had already fostered a number of children, including two young brothers named James and Kevin who came to us with lots of problems. Their mum had severe learning difficulties and could no longer care for them herself. She had been in a violent relationship with the boys' father. He had also physically abused James, the older of the brothers. James was quite badly damaged by the trauma and could vividly remember his father throwing things at him and shouting loudly in the house. Kevin was slightly more fortunate as he could not recall any of this, being a small baby when his father left the family home. David and I spent a lot of time building up James's confidence in particular. Both of the boys had learning difficulties; Kevin also had a speech impediment and they regularly soiled themselves (a common occurrence with abused children). I remember the day they arrived, and we had sat down at the table to have lunch following a (much needed) bath! As they were eating hungrily, Kevin looked at me and said, 'Elen, I tirty now.' Smiling at him, I tried to reassure him. 'No, you aren't Kevin. You have had a bath. You are lovely and clean.' Kevin just looked at me and tried again. 'I am tirty!' he insisted. Again I told him that he wasn't dirty at all. This conversation continued on and off for about fifteen minutes. Eventually James looked up at me and said. 'He is thirsty. He needs another drink!'

I like to think we helped James and Kevin to overcome some of their problems during their stay with us. In the end however, it was felt that they needed a home where they were the only children and could expect their carer's undivided attention. This was tricky in our household with Cate at such a young age and Jordan at an important point in her schooling.

The boys moved on, and next, we found ourselves providing a home for a sixteen-year-old girl by the name of

Louise and her gorgeous baby, Jade. They had been living with us for almost five months and fitted in with our family and lifestyle. Louise was delightful, funny and easy going, and the care she gave to little Jade was second to none. The only reason she had found herself caught up in the care system was because her own mum had not been able to offer an appropriate home to Louise and her tiny daughter.

I was not particularly happy with the way Louise was being treated by children's services. During the time she had lived with us she had already proved herself more capable of being a parent than many women twice her age. Nevertheless, the overall plan was to place her and her infant in a "Welcare Parenting Assessment Unit", an establishment that monitored the residents on a twenty-four hour basis, and was located a fair distance away from Louise's family as well as from us. This upset us, as we did not believe there was any need for such stringent measures, and both David and I thought she should have been given the opportunity to set up home with her boyfriend and get on with her life. The truth was, I also felt slighted that my observations of Louise had not been sufficient to influence the local authority's decision. I could not see the difference between me observing Louise or a staff member at the mother and baby unit. Surely I was just as qualified to judge? But my opinion seemed to be irrelevant. The powers that be had made their decision, and no amount of letter writing, phone calls or anything else had changed their minds, and so we were all rather unhappily waiting for a place to become available at Welcare.

Dan was still our supervising support worker, and when he telephoned me that morning, I instantly knew something important was up as he began the conversation with, 'Helen, I know you said no more babies but you are really good with them and you've got loads of experience with little 'uns. Helen, my other carers won't touch this.'

Oh dear! Dan was quite evidently trying to talk me into

accepting another baby placement. I still looked back on my experience with Timothy as having had a huge impact on me and the rest of my family, even though I never regretted that I had been lucky enough to care for him. I did not feel emotionally strong enough to go through anything similar all over again.

'He's lovely Helen, only five months old. He is so gorgeous!'

What could I do? I did not want to imagine any small baby being unwanted; I was well aware that lots of foster carers were reluctant to take them because of the work and restrictions involved.

So in the end I agreed, and it was rapidly arranged that this little baby boy would be brought to our home at about three that afternoon. Dan assured me that this placement would be fairly short term. He told me that he clearly understood my feelings about bonding with another baby and having to see that child move on. I asked him how long short term was likely to be.

'About six months,' he replied.

It seemed reasonable and I felt that we, as a family, could probably handle that; knowing that we were working to a timescale would help us to protect ourselves to some extent from becoming too emotionally attached to another baby.

I put the telephone down and immediately called David who at that time owned and ran a fish and chip shop in a nearby town. I was a bit ashamed of myself for not consulting him first. His reaction was to calmly tell me that I was insane, but that he would support whatever decision I made.

A real vote of confidence. 'Thanks David!'

The remainder of the morning passed in a blur. I had to organise our bedroom to accommodate a second cot; realised that there wasn't really any room to do that, so moved Cate's cot into the nursery, which had been ready for over a year but hardly used because I preferred to keep her close to me at night. Cate seemed puzzled watching Louise and me move her bed to the smaller room. I explained to her that a little baby was coming to live with us for a while and she seemed to accept that, although I wondered how she would feel when it was bedtime. Next, with Louise's help, I quickly began sorting through baby sheets and blankets; I unpacked the Milton sterilising unit that I had bought for Timothy; I made up some sterilising fluid and popped in the Avent bottles that had been stored in the cupboard ever since Cate had rejected them with a swift but determined "Yaaaaahhhhh" when she was a few months old. I had only bought ten of them! I knew that one day they would come in handy.

Suddenly it was 3pm and there was a knock on the front door. It was not Dan, who had been called to attend an emergency meeting, but a female colleague of his who would sign the necessary paperwork and be on hand for the baby's arrival. At ten past the hour the doorbell rang again and I rushed to answer it. This time it was Jordan returning from her friend's house. I broke the news to her as gently as I could, remembering her heartache when Timothy left us. Her response could only be described as subdued; she was probably trying to shield herself from any more hurt. Who could blame her?

The bell rang again. This time, looking dejected and with her head held low, Jordan answered the door. I was standing in the kitchen doorway watching her. 'Oh no,' I thought, 'I really do not want to see Jordan upset again because of a choice I have made.' Then I saw the baby car seat on the flagstones outside the front door. The sweetest, plumpest, "smiliest" little baby boy was staring up at Jordan, cooing and gurgling for all he was worth. What's more, Jordan, a huge smile on her face, was doing the same right back at him!

The social worker in tow was called Hannah. It was quite clear that she had no desire to spend lots of time discussing Dale's situation with me, and so the paperwork was hurriedly dealt with. I quickly scanned some of the documents and learned that when Dale was newborn, he had been placed with a foster family for the first couple of months of his life. He was then reunited with his biological mother and she was given the opportunity to prove that she could care for her son. Unfortunately, she couldn't, and he was once more taken from her. So here he was, in his third home, and still only five months old. Whilst I was trying to gain some understanding of Dale's background, Jordan and Louise crouched on the floor next to this jolly baby, totally transfixed by his charm. My own little angel, Cate, was also mesmerised by the new arrival. She kept stroking his head gently and asking if she could cuddle him. All the while Dale was making cute little noises and chuckling. He was such a darling – alert and happy, with big blue eyes and dark blonde hair that looked as though it would have a tendency to curl when it grew a little longer.

Hannah had very little background information about Dale apart from the brief outline in the documentation. Foster carers are expected to work with very few facts, to nurture, love and encourage these children, and then often, months later, will discover horrendous details about their background. In Dale's case, I heard that his mum had numerous issues connected to drugs. At no point did I read, nor was I told, how this had affected Dale himself. Finally, I signed all the necessary documents and Hannah rose to her feet to leave. I looked around the kitchen for any of this little boy's belongings. Hannah told me that she had forgotten to bring them from her car. She strolled down the drive, her long skirt skimming the ground and came back with a small black holdall. There was not much in it: some grubby vests, a couple of T-shirts and jogging bottoms, a cymbal-playing Tigger, a black and white toy dog with a name tag, which said "Merry" and a rather tatty looking yellow and blue elephant. Surprisingly, there were also three pairs of leather trainers. One pair was Adidas, one was Nike and the other a Disney Winnie the Pooh. Obviously someone cared passionately about this child's feet! Hannah informed me that Dale was taking six ounces of SMA Gold formula milk and had already started solids. And then she was gone, with a final shimmy of her skirt and a shake of her large gold hoop earrings. The social worker who was standing in for Dan followed close on her heels.

I looked around the kitchen. Two sixteen-year-old girls, three babies aged twenty-four, five and four months, our Labrador, Fudge, and me! Jordan asked if she could take Dale out of his car seat. I was very pleased but also somewhat surprised. Jordan had totally withdrawn from any involvement with babies – including her own sister – since Timothy went. Now, she was asking to hold our new arrival. I nodded enthusiastically and watched as she carefully lifted Dale and held him tight. Dale was totally delighted; he snuggled into Jordan's shoulder and tugged at her long hair. Cate would not have got away with that. Now Jordan was smiling and talking to this little boy as though it was the most natural thing in the world. I had certainly not foreseen this, but it was a truly heart-warming sight and I suddenly felt that I had definitely made the right decision about this placement.

As Louise was busying herself with Jade, I thought it would be nice to take our latest charge to visit David at the chip shop. I changed Dale's rather damp bottom, fed him his formula milk and then popped him, quite relaxed, into the car. Jordan and Cate got in too and off we went. Dale was in the front seat, facing Jordan in the back. He gurgled and smiled for the whole of the thirty-minute journey and Jordan chatted and smiled right back at him. Cate was understandably more than a little bemused. She had never seen her sister so animated.

David's initial meeting with Dale was unremarkable. We

arrived at "David's Plaice" and trooped into the shop. Evening trade had begun and David was already busy serving. The cuddle was quick and rather greasy; then Dale was passed back to me so that we could visit a nearby store to pick up some new clothes for him. The baby was completely shattered by this time. His big blue eyes were closing, his long lashes brushing his chubby cheeks, as he tried hard to fight off sleep. By the time we got home he was out for the count and even changing him into his new pyjamas didn't wake him. As I lay him down in the cot at the foot of my bed, he began to whimper quietly. I lifted him out and soothed him and soon he was gently snoring and seemed to be smiling in his sleep. Once he was tucked up in the cot, he slept soundly all night, even when Cate woke up and came into our bed for what was to become a traditional cuddle every night. What a good boy.

Next morning, a cheery Dale was awake by 8am. He ate his breakfast with relish and drank down his milk, then contentedly watched us all in the kitchen getting ready for the day ahead. David did not have much time to spend with us as he always left early to prepare and organise food at the chip shop for the lunchtime rush. Jordan had already made plans to spend the day shopping with her friend Rosie. She left too – but not before kissing her new foster brother on his downy head. He immediately beamed and reached for her, and in response Jordan ruffled his hair with affection. I hoped this new placement might go some way to help her recover from the ordeal of losing Timothy. Having Dale in the house could be a positive step in the healing process, not just for Jordan but also for me. Dale's arrival seemed to herald a good time for all of us.

Cate, Louise, Jade and I spent the next few hours getting to know Dale. He was one of the happiest babies I had ever seen, constantly smiling and chuckling at things going on around him. He was also a very active child, picking up anything and everything he could get his hands on and examining it closely. It was plain to see, even at that very young age, that his fingers were strong and he was really dexterous. He, Cate and Jade had lots of fun playing with the baby gyms we had in the house. Dale was huge compared with little Jade who had been born prematurely and was a dainty little thing. He soon learned that with a little effort he could roll himself towards Jade and he endeavoured to do this whenever possible. Louise and I had to watch him very carefully as he could easily have rolled right over her.

Louise made me laugh when she sang, *'Dale, Dale, Oh Dale the snail!'*, then grinned and said, *'that is really silly as you're nothing like a snail are you? Oh I know, Dale the Whale!'*

I have to say, that name has stuck.

The day passed in a blur of bottles, bibs and burps and soon it was time to lay weary heads in cots and prepare for the next day when we would start all over again.

How wrong I was to be so pleased. Next morning a telephone call came to say that a place had been found at Welcare for Louise and Jade. The irony was that when we accepted Dale, we freed up a place at the parent and baby unit that had been his home for the past three months. Louise and Jade would be moving into the very room that Dale and his birth mother had vacated. Louise was distraught that she was to leave us. I admit that we both sat around the kitchen table and cried. When I had composed myself sufficiently to speak to someone, I telephoned the children's services department responsible for Louise and Jade. I realised that they expected Louise to find her own way to Welcare with Jade and all their belongings. Not an easy task for a sixteen-year-old mother with no access to a car apart from mine, which could not accommodate three babies. I was exasperated and tried to negotiate on Louise's behalf. I explained that it was quite impossible for Louise to move without some help and I was not allowing her to leave my care until I was certain she would be safe. The duty social worker sighed and reluctantly agreed that Louise could arrange transport with her sister's boyfriend, Eddie, who owned a taxicab, and that they would pay.

Arrangements tentatively in place, Louise and I turned to the task in hand and began to pack. It was quite a job. It's surprising how much a teenager and a baby can accumulate in just five months. Also, David and I, fully expecting that Louise and Jade would in due course leave us to move to their own flat, had begun collecting various household items for her such as cutlery, crockery and even a toaster. The room at Welcare was on the small side but would contain most of what she required. Therefore lots of her possessions needed to be boxed and labelled for storage at one of her sisters' homes, ready for the day when she and Jade would leave the unit.

It was only two days later when Eddie arrived in his minicab to transport Louise and Jade to Welcare. We would miss them greatly. It was another sad day for us all.

❋ ❋ ❋

It was also quite a shock to be looking after two small and very active children without help, now that Louise was gone. David was rarely at home as the chip shop was occupying most of his time. I was reluctant to ask Jordan to give up her leisure time, and secretly I was also afraid of her bonding too much with Dale. Every second of my day revolved around little ones demanding my attention; it was absolutely chaotic but at the same time very rewarding and lots of fun. Dale was such a gorgeous baby. He was extremely easy going and his laughter was always in my ears because he found just about everything funny. Cate adjusted very well to Dale's arrival. While she obviously missed Louise and Jade, Dale helped fill the gap they had left. Even though he was nineteen months younger than Cate, Dale was quite big for his age, and the two of them seemed to enjoy spending time together, watching videos or playing with some toy or the other. Cate also liked the fact that she was older than him and began to mother him, regularly kissing him on the cheek and telling me how cute he was.

Of course Jordan did help out as much as she possibly could, and the four of us spent some happy hours together visiting the shopping centre or sitting in the garden enjoying the sun. We quickly learned how to handle the gigantic double buggy we had bought to accommodate both small children, and got used to yet another way of life. We were happy to know that Louise and Jade were doing very well and hoped that they would soon be allowed to leave Welcare to be re-housed in the area where her family lived and nearer to us

Weeks turned into months, and although there were some days when I felt almost overwhelmed, Dale's smile and both my daughters' obvious affection for him kept me going.

3

Time goes on

When Dale had been with us for almost six months, there was still no sign of an adoptive family for him. I had always been led to believe, by our own foster agency, that he was absolutely certain to be placed for adoption, but little or no action seemed to have been taken to set the wheels in motion. His birth mum had not made very much of an effort to have contact, and had, in fact, only seen him twice since he was removed from her care. On one of those occasions Dale had come back in a completely different outfit to the one I had dressed him in that morning. That in itself was not really unusual; parents whose children are in care often try to retain some control by changing their children's clothes. It normally didn't bother me. This time, however, I was upset. I had sent Dale out in a pair of shorts and a cotton T-shirt. The day was extremely hot, and because he was such an active child, he needed to be kept cool. Hannah brought Dale back in her car with the midday sun blazing through the windows. When I took him out of his car seat he was dripping with sweat and even his hair was plastered to his head. His cheeks were bright red and he was obviously distressed. He was wearing a pale blue woollen suit over a long sleeved cotton jersey. While I began to strip him, Hannah tried to explain that Mum wanted Dale to wear these clothes to contact from now on. I gasped as I removed the cotton jersey. Underneath was a thick vest.

'How could you let her dress him in such warm clothes?' I asked, astounded.

'Well, it was only for a short time,' was her excuse. 'He will be fine.'

'Let's hope so,' I retorted.

Hannah did not seem to be concerned that, in the middle of a hot summer, Dale's mum had decided to dress him in totally inappropriate clothes as a means to exert her right as his mother.

The next time Dale's mum was due to have contact, Hannah arrived again to pick him up. It was yet another sweltering day and I had him all ready to go. He was looking beautiful in a pair of cotton, short-leg dungarees with a pale blue T-shirt underneath.

'Have you got his shoes and socks?' Hannah asked.

I stared at her in disbelief.

'Why, is he walking to contact?'

Hannah patiently explained that Dale's mum had specifically asked that he wore the shoes she had provided.

'No way!' I answered.

'For a start, they no longer fit him properly. Secondly, you can tell his mum that it is not recommended for babies to wear shoes on their feet until they are walking.'

Hannah began to argue.

'Yes, I understand how you feel but Mum wants him to wear shoes.'

'I don't care,' I said firmly, 'I am not saying it to be difficult Hannah. It is actually the advice given by children's shoe specialists.'

'Well, at least put socks on him then.'

'Fine,' I retorted, 'but he doesn't really need them in this heat.'

The irony of it was that Dale's mum didn't even show up that day and Dale was returned home within the hour. The first thing I did when Hannah brought him into the house was remove the socks from his hot little feet.

A couple more contact sessions were arranged and each time, Hannah picked up Dale only to return him unexpectedly because his mum did not show up at the family centre where contact was supposed to take place. I found this very distressing because it was unsettling for Dale. I noticed that he would start to cry as soon as Hannah carried him down the drive to her car, and it seemed he was being upset for no good reason, as it was unlikely his mum would even show up. Then I got a call from Dale's children's guardian, appointed by the court, who arranged to visit. Whilst we were sitting having a cup of tea together, I mentioned that Dale's mum was failing to attend contact sessions and therefore wasn't spending time with her little boy.

'I think it's very hard for her,' Caroline told me. 'She has had two other sons taken into care and they have already been adopted. Now Dale has been taken from her too. In her heart I think she knows she won't get him back. This was her last chance to prove she could be a good mother and she failed.'

'But surely she could at least try? She could turn up for contact and show everybody that she really does care.'

I was taken aback that any mother would simply give up and not put up some sort of a fight for her child.

But Caroline said, 'She doesn't have any of your advantages, Helen. She has very little education and nobody to turn to for support. I think she feels helpless and alone – especially as she has now separated from Dale's dad.'

I started feeling sad for this faceless woman who would yet again lose a son to adoption. I didn't want Dale to be returned to her if she was unable to care for him and neglect him, but I could imagine how terrible she must feel inside, knowing that someone else would raise her little boy, and that once he went to an adoptive family, she would probably never cuddle or kiss him again whilst he was small. As it happened, Dale's mum never turned up to see her son again. However, her own mother did get in touch with the local authority in an attempt to see her grandson, but due to unspecified problems between her and her daughter, children's services needed to ask Dale's mum's permission. I was told they tried to contact her by phone and letter but failed to trace her. She had moved from the hostel she had been living in and slipped off the radar. I was informed that there would be no contact sessions with any of Dale's birth family from then on until further notice. I had mixed feelings about this. On the one hand, it seemed so sad that Dale would be deprived of connections to his blood relatives. On the other hand, I felt a sense of relief that there would be no further need to send him off to the family centre for a contact session that might never take place.

Dale's circumstances seemed rather odd to me. I had always been told that there was no possibility of him returning to his mum, and I usually found that young children, and especially babies, who had no chance of going back to their birth families, were placed for adoption quite quickly. I began to wonder about the reasons for the delay in Dale's case. Nothing was moving forward and there was no preparation for the time he would join a new and permanent family. I questioned Dan, our support worker, but he had no more idea than I did of the reason behind the hold-up. It was very strange. I also felt that I needed to remind Dan of how we had initially discussed the length of time Dale would stay with us. I explained again how I was afraid of becoming too attached to him. Whilst Dan was sympathetic, he had no real solution. He told me that he had been honest when he said the placement would be short term as that was the information he had been given. However, he admitted that very often placements did not stick to the planned time scale and that I would need to be patient. Of course I understood, but I felt uneasy thinking ahead to the time I would need to say goodbye to Dale.

By mid-autumn, David and I decided to ask the local authority responsible for Dale if we could take him with us to our holiday home in Florida. We were planning to go just after Christmas 2004, together with my parents, and I could not imagine allowing anyone else to look after Dale while we went away without him. The alarm bells should have been sounding at this point, as I know numerous carers who have no trouble placing their foster children in respite care while they enjoy a family holiday. For me however, this was not an option; I was already too attached to this little boy even to consider it. In any case, there was no problem getting permission to take him with us. Dan told us that children's services would much prefer to pay for a passport than arrange respite care, which was both disruptive for the child and expensive. I discovered that Dale's social worker, Hannah, had moved to another area, and Dale now had someone new named Carla. I was quite glad as I never felt Hannah and I really saw eye to eye about many things connected to Dale's care. I just hoped that I would find Carla easier to get along with. When I spoke to her about taking Dale on a holiday she quickly agreed to organise a passport if I supplied her with current photographs.

We booked our flights for the 27th of December. Our plan was to drive to Gatwick on Boxing Day, where we had reserved two hotel rooms for the night. It was a pretty frenzied run-up to Christmas Day; I fretted over just about everything including packing, presents, travel sickness and the children's reaction to such a lengthy journey. You name it, I thought up an anxious scenario to go with it. For a full week before we were due to travel, our suitcases were open on the upstairs landing and I was constantly packing and re-packing to check I had not forgotten anything. Regardless of this, we had a fun-filled Christmas Day with both small children being totally overwhelmed by all the new toys. Already able to walk at only ten months, Dale's favourite game that day was squeezing into the box that had held his Mega Brick fire engine. His squeals of laughter each time we were "surprised" to discover his hiding place filled the air.

Suddenly though, Boxing Day was upon us and my parents arrived as arranged to pick up Jordan and drive her to the airport. Predictably, I was still not ready to leave the house. I was getting more and more agitated over the trip and I was transferring that worry to the children, who were both clingy and miserable. We eventually left the house at 5pm. Our luggage was jammed into the back of David's Cherokee Jeep along with our Labrador, Fudge, who was being taken to my brother's home for the night. He had agreed to take her to the kennels when they re-opened the following day, after the Christmas break. We finally left there at about 6pm just as the phone call came from my parents trying to establish where we were. They were already waiting at the hotel.

In due course we did make it to Gatwick with both Cate and Dale in pretty wretched shape, and David and I hardly speaking because we felt so stressed out. It was not the best start to our holiday and sadly things would not improve.

Once on board the aircraft early next morning, we were grilled by an overly suspicious air-hostess about Cate's wellbeing, and whether or not permission would be granted for her to fly. With the excitement of Christmas and the tension of the journey to the airport, her eczema had flared up with a vengeance, and the flight crew suspected chicken pox. I patiently explained to the cabin crew and security that my daughter was in no way contagious. Once I had convinced everyone of that fact, we were allowed to fly out of Gatwick, heading for Cincinnati where we would catch our connecting flight to Orlando International Airport. On the plane I glimpsed a newspaper headline about a tragedy in Asia but it would be two days before any of us became aware that the tsunami had struck the coast of Indonesia, killing over two hundred thousand people.

True to form, our arrival in Cincinnati was not straightforward. There was some dispute with American luggage handlers and we were all perturbed to see our suitcases thrown into a multi-coloured, jam-packed stockpile of personal belongings. We considered the possibility that we might never see our luggage again and tried (but, I have to confess, failed) to see the funny side. Little did we know that when we finally touched down in Florida, our bags would be heading in a totally different direction. Not even Dale's buggy made it. We were forced to sit and wait in the airport foyer whilst jostling, angry and tired passengers demanded answers from the airport staff who, in the main, were tight lipped and unwilling to give anything away. Fortunately we had some blankets and jumpers in our hand luggage, and my mum and I made the children as comfortable as we could, while David and my father attempted to find out where our luggage might be.

Eventually we simply collected the hired vehicle and headed for the villa, leaving the luggage problem behind until the morning. Even that could not be straightforward. We got into the car, and I lay Dale on the back seat and reached for the seatbelt, only to find a small pack of prescription drugs concealed there. I realised that one of the children could have found it and swallowed a pill. By this time I was feeling close to tears.

Arriving at the villa an hour later was something of a relief. Everything looked clean and tidy and we immediately got the exhausted youngsters tucked up in their beds. David, Jordan and I then headed off to the nearby Wal-Mart for emergency supplies. Surely nothing else could go wrong?

As it turned out, the holiday was as close to a disaster as we could have imagined. Everyone except Jordan went down with an unpleasant virus that caused sickness and headaches. Cate's eczema refused to be controlled by the usual creams and emollients and I lost count of the people who stopped me to ask sympathetically if she was a burns victim. Dale regressed into the clingiest child I had ever dealt with and absolutely refused to let me out of his sight, screaming for Britain if I so much as handed him over to my mother to go to the toilet. Furthermore, my mother and David decided to unashamedly rub each other up the wrong way for the duration of our stay. I began questioning the wisdom of a joint holiday and seriously considered trying to get an immediate flight out of Florida.

Two days after our arrival, following a marathon stake-out at the airport by David and Dad, most of our luggage, including the buggy, resurfaced. It didn't make much difference really, as in my ultimate wisdom I had packed most of our new Christmas clothes, which were obviously winter wear, and Florida was experiencing freak temperatures in the high eighties. On top of that, one day before we set off to the shopping mall, David succeeded in reversing our hire car over Dale's buggy. Luckily it survived the incident as I couldn't bring myself to tell my mother what had happened lest she physically attack my husband.

The final straw came when we were behind schedule leaving the villa to travel back to the airport; we got lost on the way and eventually screeched up to the terminal at 2pm for a 2.30pm departure. I was breathless:

'The Gatwick flight....? Are we too late?'

The representative was calm.

'No honey, you have heaps of time. It doesn't depart until 6pm.'

'The Monarch 312?' I clarified, panting hard.

'Oh my God!' Realisation struck like a thunderbolt as she saw the rest of the party rushing towards her dragging a variety of luggage and kids. On reflection, our luck began to turn at that moment. I burst into tears, and I imagine the danger of me having some sort of breakdown at her feet persuaded her to contact the boarding gate. Fortune smiled on us finally, and the Captain, obviously a very compassionate man, agreed to allow us to be rushed through all necessary controls in order to make that flight home.

I can honestly say that I have never been so totally delighted to see the end of a holiday.

Once home and settled into a routine again, the horror of our calamitous Florida experience faded, leaving surprisingly few scars. Days drifted by and Dale's first birthday was approaching. I organised a small party for family and friends at home, with lots of entertainment and laughter. Even my mum and David appeared to have put any evil thoughts they may have had about each other aside, and were almost chummy again. The day after the party, Dale was in the hallway playing with Cate when I heard a sharp cry. Dale came toddling towards me with a frightened look on his face.

'What's wrong little man?' I asked him smiling. Then to my horror, I saw his lips were turning blue and his eyes were starting to flutter closed. I managed to catch him just as he slumped to the floor. I screamed, absolutely terrified, for David who rushed into the room, took one look at the situation and grabbed Dale from me. He began slapping his back; I tried to peer into Dale's mouth as my first thought was that he was choking on something. There was nothing to be seen and Dale's face was a horrible grey colour. All my first aid training flew from my mind. Crying and shaking, I grabbed the phone and punched 999. I told the operator that Dale was not breathing. David in the meantime had set off at a run down the street to our neighbour, a local GP. The operator tried to calm me down, assuring me that a First Response Paramedic was already on his way. I ran into the garden shouting frantically for Diane my immediate next door neighbour. There was no answer from her house and neither could I see David at the doctor's house. I have never been so scared in my life; I honestly thought Dale was dead. I had even forgotten about poor Cate who, when I re-entered the house, had not moved from the hallway where she had been playing with Dale. I scooped her into my arms and ran out of the front door. Suddenly, across the road at my friend Vanessa's house I saw a gathering of people. There was David, and thank God, Dale was upright in his arms and I heard the beautiful sound of him crying.

Later, David told me that he had given him mouth to mouth outside the doctor's house when he had failed to get an answer. He had then rushed to Vanessa's, who was a nurse, but luckily Dale had already begun to show signs of recovery. The paramedic, who arrived at that moment with sirens blaring, quickly checked a very subdued and pale Dale. Then the ambulance crew arrived and they too examined him. I was almost hysterical with fear and relief all mixed together and was shaking uncontrollably. It was decided to take Dale to the hospital to ensure that all was well as no obvious cause could be found for his collapse.

By the time we were in the back of the ambulance, Dale was already pulling medical equipment around and being his usual inquisitive self. I was petrified that he had some unidentified medical condition. The ambulance men considered giving me oxygen as I appeared to need it more than Dale.

We never found out what caused Dale's collapse that day. It was suggested that he may have fallen over and winded himself when he was playing in the hallway, although he had no bump or scrape, and Cate was too young to be able to tell us what happened. The doctor at the hospital said when we slapped his back we could even have winded him more and made things worse. Other possible scenarios were put forward but we have had to accept that we do not know what happened and probably never will. I just pray that we never experience anything as frightening again.

* * *

Following the shock of Dale's mishap, my thoughts began to turn to the time when I would receive the phone call from social services telling me that an adoptive family had been identified for Dale. I felt distressed at the very idea, but I told myself that this had always been the plan and I needed to be professional and work with that. Weeks went past and suddenly, February was over and we still had no further information about a permanent home for Dale.

David had decided that he was not seeing enough of the children. The fish and chip shop, whilst making us a living, was never going to make our fortunes. For the number of hours David was putting into it, the returns were not enough. So, after some careful thought we decided to put it on the market and sell it as a going concern. Luckily, a young man expressed an interest almost immediately as he was keen to start his own business. His parents were already in the restaurant trade and a deal on David's Plaice was quickly struck.

By mid-March I was beginning to have terrible difficulty imagining the day when I would have to hand Dale over to new parents. A tiny little thought had begun to worm its way into my head and, however hard I tried to ignore it, it just would not go away. I began to wonder how my family would react if I suddenly announced that I would like us to adopt Dale. When we were looking after Timothy, our first ever foster child, one of the senior social workers assigned to his case suggested more than once that we put ourselves forward to adopt him. I had been very tempted but David, always more practical and less emotional than me, had tried to discourage me. In the end I could see his point of view: we had only just started fostering and we could not adopt every single child I formed a bond with. And now, three years down the line, there was Dale's future to decide. There were many other people and factors to think about apart from the initial hurdle of David's reaction. For a start, there was Dale's new social worker, Carla, who could be totally against the idea. I felt it might be a good move to approach her and seek out her feelings first, so I telephoned her and tentatively broached the subject. Her reaction astonished and heartened me.

'You are marvellous,' she said. 'How wonderful, fantastic! I think it would be a great idea.'

Carla went on to tell me how to put my plan into action and gave me a contact name and address to write to in order to set the wheels in motion.

I was thrilled as I knew of other foster carers who had tried and failed to go down this path. Many had been stopped immediately in their tracks by being told categorically that an application from them would not be considered. In particular, one friend of mine who fostered for the same independent agency had accepted a baby placement a year earlier. Quickly becoming attached to the little boy, Lily and her husband spoke to his social worker about applying to adopt him. They received a very different response from the one I had from Carla. They were told that they should be grateful that they already had children of their own, and that there were people out there unable to conceive and longing to be parents. This very thought had crossed my mind as we already had Jordan and Cate, but Carla had not seen that as an obstacle, so at least I felt that I stood a chance, and that very night, I decided to talk to David about adding to our family.

I was very nervous when David got home at the end of

his shift at the fish shop. I was trembling and however hard I tried to bring up the subject of adoption, I could not find the words. I feared that due to David's long working hours, he had not really had the opportunity to bond with Dale in the same way that I had. I also knew that David felt bringing up two daughters was hard enough financially without adding another child. But I could no longer imagine Dale not being part of the family. I had grown to love him so much, and I wanted us to raise him as our son and a brother to Jordan and Cate. Thinking of the conversation that I would need to have with my husband, I told myself that I was more than ready for a fight. In the event, I never really anticipated what a battle it was going to turn into to.

4

Asking to adopt

I finally managed to pluck up the courage to speak to David about what was on my mind. His answer could only be described as low-key. He thought his refusal to consider adopting Timothy had led to some difficulties in our relationship and made me unhappy; he would therefore support whatever decision I made. On the one hand, I was delighted because I felt I could go ahead and let the local authority know what I wanted to do, but on the other, I felt troubled as I sensed David was agreeing to my plan for all the wrong reasons. I still wasn't sure about his feelings for Dale and I knew that if he was going to become our son on a permanent basis, he would need to be treated and loved in the same way as Jordan and Cate. Still, I felt I had made some progress, so I asked the rest of the family how they felt about us adopting Dale. My mum and dad and brothers all encouraged us; Jordan, as expected, was supportive, but David's parents were slightly less enthusiastic. They didn't come out with anything negative, but I had the feeling that they thought it was quite a strange thing to want to do. However, they had always treated all our foster children very lovingly and I hoped they would soon start to view Dale as a "proper" grandson and not just one on loan from social services.

With the family more or less on board, I turned to the really important matter: that of formalising our application to adopt. On April 8th 2005, I took Carla's advice and put into writing our request to be considered as prospective adopters for Dale. This was my letter to the adoption team of my local authority:

Dear Sir/Madam
I write in order to request that my husband and I be considered as adoptive parents for the little boy we are currently fostering. His name is Dale Anthony xxxxx and he was placed with us on July 28th 2004 by xxxxx Social Services.

To tell you a little bit about ourselves, my husband David and I first met in 1996 and married in the Dominican Republic in the year 2001. I already had one daughter, Jordan, from a previous relationship and in 2002 another daughter, Cate, was born to us. We have fostered for our independent agency since January 2002, and we have shared our home with numerous children of varying age groups since then. Prior to becoming a foster mum, I worked for the health authority in a clerical capacity and my employment history – in the UK – since leaving school has always revolved around administration in the NHS. When I was in my early twenties, I moved to Spain with my family and remained there for a number of years. My eldest daughter's keen ear for languages, and indeed her excellent communication skills, reflect this experience. On my return to the UK, I decided to continue my education and became an undergraduate at the University of Glamorgan where I gained my BA (Hons) in English in 1999.

David's trade is in carpentry and he was employed until late October 2002 as the General Manager of a furniture frame-making company in our local area. On resigning from his post after nine years, he decided to open a business of his own. In 2003 he purchased a property and launched a fish and chip takeaway. Earlier this year he sold that business and is in the process of deciding his next venture.

Jordan is now aged 17 and is currently a sixth form student after achieving outstanding GCSE results. Her intention is to go on to university where she hopes to study for a career in Law. Cate, aged two-and-a-half, will begin school in September 2005.

David and I own our own home. It is a four-bedroom detached property in a semi-rural position. We also own a home in Florida, which we rent out to holiday makers and use ourselves whenever we need a break. We feel that we can offer Dale a stable and loving environment where he will be given exactly the same opportunities as Jordan and Cate. He is a wonderful child to care for, happy and contented, and he is an important part of our lives. He and Cate in particular have bonded as brother and sister and I think they will miss each other dreadfully if they are separated. My own parents as well as David's treat Dale as a grandson and he is further cherished by our respective brothers and their families. We all love Dale very much and ask that we can be given the chance to raise him as part of our family.

I look forward to hearing from you with regard to our next step in this process and hope that you look favourably upon this request.

Yours sincerely
Helen Jayne

I sealed the envelope and posted it the same day to the adoption department. Then I sat back and waited.

* * *

Friday April 15th 2005. The postman knocked at the door with a handful of letters. Cate and Dale were quietly watching television, so I sat down at the kitchen table with a cup of tea and began to go through the mail. One envelope caught my attention as it was franked with the local authority's name and logo. Feeling excited, I tore the envelope open and scanned the contents. Then, with a sinking heart, I re-read the letter in an attempt to take it in. In a nutshell, I was being told that David and I were not going to be considered as adoptive parents because we were foster carers and, as such, we were being turned down as potential adopters for Dale. The letter stated that 'no decision has been made as to whether adoption is in the child's best interests'. It went on, 'should such a decision be made, then we have existing available approved families who are awaiting a placement'.

I could not believe it, and with shaking hands and a pounding heart, I folded the letter up and put it in the drawer. I felt completely devastated and the rest of the day passed in a blur. I was not really sure what I should do next and I didn't feel up to discussing the letter with anyone as I was so upset. I didn't understand why we were not going to be considered as adoptive parents as there was no clear reason given in the letter. I did not feel the fact that there were carers already approved should influence what was the best decision for Dale. David and I were applying to be assessed specifically for Dale, and I was sure that there were plenty of other children waiting to be adopted in the UK. It made no sense to me.

When David came home from the fish shop that night I forced myself to share the disappointing news with him. David's response was to shrug his shoulders in total acceptance of the situation. That infuriated me. I became angry and lost my temper and a heated argument followed, with me ranting and raving about the unfairness of it all until the tears came. David, seeing how upset I was, tried his best to comfort me but his reaction to what I had viewed as the worst possible news, made me unreasonable and I didn't want to give him the chance to make me feel better. That night I cried myself to sleep.

Next morning I rang my mum and ran through the events of the previous day with her. She asked me what I intended to do. I began to think through the options that might be available to me. If my mother thought something could be done then maybe there was still hope. I had already mulled over some possibilities during the night and wondered if I should take advice from our fostering agency before making any further attempt to contact the adoption team.

My mum agreed that it was a sensible approach and her encouragement spurred me on. As it was the weekend I knew I couldn't reach anyone until Monday so I prepared a list of questions that I wanted to put to my new support worker. Dan had recently changed jobs within the company and we had been assigned to a woman named Jean. I was not looking forward to speaking to her about adopting Dale because, when I had first mentioned the possibility, her response had been very unenthusiastic. In a way, I understood: the agency had invested both time and money training us to care for children that the local authority were unable to place, and here we were talking about providing a permanent home for Dale, using one of our bedrooms that could otherwise accommodate another foster child in need. I had tried to explain that we would continue to foster even if we did successfully adopt Dale but detected the scepticism in Jean's voice. I knew that my next conversation with her would be difficult.

Monday morning arrived and I nervously dialled our agency's telephone number. I was quickly put through to

Jean and told her about the letter from the adoption agency. I got very little sympathy. Instead, she explained that the organisation could not be seen to support our application to adopt as they had a contract with the local authority to provide foster placements for the children referred to them. She went on to say that she could offer emotional support but she could not back our wish to make Dale a permanent part of our family. Even though I had anticipated this reply, I still felt let down and told Jean so. She coolly acknowledged my feelings but explained again that the only advice she could give me was to write once more to the local authority adoption department. I immediately sat down and wrote a second short letter asking that our request be reconsidered. That done, I hoped determination would be enough to get us where we wanted, and I tried to get on with my life.

In the meantime I had plenty to keep me occupied. We had accepted another foster placement, a teenage boy, who was keeping us on our toes as he liked nothing better than wandering the streets in the early hours with his friends on the look out for cars to steal. We often had police officers at our door, with him in tow, and that succeeded slightly in taking my mind off the rejection, although Dale, and what the future held for him, and for us, was never very far from my thoughts.

More than a week went by before I heard anything at all. I kept telling myself that no news was good news and kept my fingers crossed that it was true! Then a second letter arrived.

> *Dear Ms Jayne*
> *Thank you for your letter, which we received on 20 April. We note the contents and will write to you again in due course.*
>
> *Yours sincerely*
> *Adoption Manager*

I was a bit puzzled by this letter, which told me very little but hoped that the authority was considering my request more thoroughly and so I sat back and waited once more. On the morning of April 28th, our support worker Jean arrived unannounced. She told us that she had been contacted by the team responsible for Dale, and they had asked her to attend a meeting the next morning in connection with my letter.

'Should David and I be there?' I asked, thinking that if there was a meeting to discuss our future then we should be part of it.

'No, you are not invited,' she replied, 'and I don't think that it will result in good news for you either, I'm afraid.' I was shaken by what she said. I had made the mistake of assuming that the lack of response from the adoption team was a positive sign but now it seemed that was not the case. I felt foolish that I had allowed myself to believe that everything would work out in our favour.

'I will come back here after the meeting tomorrow to let you know exactly where you stand,' Jean told us before she left.

True to her word, by mid-day on April 29th, Jean was once more in our kitchen looking as solemn as I had ever seen her.

'It is not good news for you, I'm sorry. A decision has been taken to remove Dale from your care immediately. social services are looking for another foster family as we speak.'

'Why?' I asked. 'I just don't understand what we have done wrong.' David put his arm around my shoulders.

'They feel you have broken the contract and on top of that, they don't think that you will be able to deal with moving him to another placement.'

'Well that's not true,' David said crossly, 'If we have to move him then we will act professionally and do our job.'

'Yes, I believe you would. But it is not me you have to

convince,' Jean replied.

By this time I was too upset to think straight. 'I'll go to the papers,' I said in desperation.

Jean frowned and shook her head. 'I don't think that is a good idea Helen. It could even make things worse for you.'

I was past caring. 'How could it be any worse?'

All I could think of was that at any time, a social worker could knock on my door and demand I hand Dale over without making a fuss. I didn't think I could do it. I began to cry. Jean, looking upset, took her leave. She and David spoke briefly at the door and then she was gone.

David told me when he came back that Jean had asked him if he thought I might try to leave the country with Dale. He had assured her that I would not do such a thing. I felt guilty because the thought had not only crossed my mind but I had even very tentatively called a friend in the US to ask if I could stay with him and his wife if I had to leave the UK in a hurry. David was horrified when I confided in him and made me realise how ridiculous I was being. I wondered at the time why social services had not simply asked to have Dale's passport back if they truly felt I might abscond. In my mind, that would have been the easiest and safest thing to do. However, I have to thank Jean for her faith in me, as I found out later that, when the question was raised, she strenuously denied that I would ever resort to that.

I decided I would pack a small bag for Dale just in case a social worker caught me unawares and I was forced to let him leave my care. I sadly put some of his familiar things, cosy pyjamas, T-shirts and shorts, a couple of bottles and a few soft toys into a bag, and put it where it would be close to hand if it was needed in a hurry.

Next morning, the expected letter from children's services arrived. I opened it and scanned the contents. One sentence immediately jumped out at me: '…the decision has been made to remove Dale from your care as soon as other suitable foster carers have been identified.'

Although I had been expecting it, the actual letter forced me to act. I could crumble and accept the fact that we would have to part with Dale, or I could point blank refuse to give up. In that instant I knew it had to be the latter. I would never forgive myself if I allowed strangers to come to my home and leave with the little boy we loved so much. I also knew that there was very little point in phoning around family and friends to tell them of the latest development. What could they do other than offer a sympathetic ear? Instead, I picked up the Yellow Pages and turned to the heading "Solicitors". As it was a bank holiday weekend, I had to wait until the following Tuesday before I could telephone a few local numbers, only to be told that they did not deal in family law. Finally, one was able to recommend a local firm which did. I rang them and learned that the solicitor I would need to speak to was in court and would not return to the office until later that day. I agreed to ring back at four o' clock and spent the rest of the day on tenterhooks. When I did call back, it was to be told that Ms Parks had not yet returned from court. The frustration was killing me. I tried the office again and eventually managed to speak to the solicitor at 5.25 in the evening – just five minutes before the office closed. I quickly explained my predicament and she agreed to make an appointment to discuss the case the following Thursday. That meant I had two days to wait before I would learn if we had a chance to fight for Dale.

The waiting was hard and I was keenly aware that my mood affected the younger children in the house quite badly. Both Cate and Dale were clingy and weepy, and Jordan was very concerned at how unhappy and upset I was. She was a rock at this point, constantly boiling the kettle and keeping me fuelled on hot cups of tea. Even our other foster son calmed down and spent more time at home, being as helpful as he could, which was a great relief to me.

However, I spent an emotional and anxious weekend even though I was certain that nothing would happen on the Saturday or Sunday as the local authority office would be closed and only duty social workers would be on call. But on Thursday morning, May 5th 2005, I received a phone call from Carla, Dale's social worker. My heart almost missed a beat when I answered the phone and heard her voice. She asked would it be OK if she visited that afternoon at 2pm to explain their decision. I unenthusiastically agreed and asked Jean to come to the meeting as well.

It was an awkward state of affairs. Carla and Jean sat side by side on one sofa whilst David and I sat on the other. Carla began to say that when they originally placed Dale with us it was on the basis that he would move on to adoptive parents. I agreed with her, but explained that when I accepted the placement it had also been on the basis that it would be a short-term arrangement for approximately six months. I pointed out that the fostering agency was completely aware of my tendency to become emotionally attached to the children I looked after – especially the tiny ones. Carla and Jean both seemed to accept this fact, but Carla continued trying to explain the adoption team's stance. I was in no mood to hear what she was saying. 'Take your social worker head off Carla and answer me this,' I said heatedly. 'Where do you honestly think Dale should be?'

She looked back at me steadily and narrowed her eyes slightly. 'Off the record?'

I nodded.

'Right here with you and David.'

I glanced triumphantly at Jean and then back at Carla.

'We are the best option for Dale. He is settled here, he loves us all and we are all he really knows. He would be distraught if someone came and took him away after all this time!'

'Children are resilient,' Jean interrupted. 'He may be upset and unsettled for a day or two but he would soon get over it.'

Now I was bristling with hostility because Jean was meant, after all, to be my support worker.

'I don't care Jean! If I could prevent him from being unhappy for a second, let alone hours or days, then I would do it!!'

Carla nodded her head sympathetically, but went on, 'Helen, we know you have provided excellent care for Dale whilst he has been here. That is not in question at all. Everybody knows you love him but part of the placement plan was for him to move on to adoption and that is why the decision was reached. The authority is just following the original plan agreed by the courts,' she said gently.

'All I have done is love him and treat him as part of my family. So why do I feel as though I've done something wrong? I am a good foster carer and I'm being penalised for doing my job well.' The tears were threatening again and I was shaking with emotion and self-righteousness. David squeezed my hand but it didn't help.

Then Jean spoke again. 'Well, you haven't really done your job, have you? At the end of the day Helen, you are a foster carer and not an adopter, so your job was only ever to provide a temporary home for Dale!'

David put a preventive arm on my shoulder as he realised I was about to rise to my feet. I restrained myself, well aware that a show of childish temper would not help my case but I could not hold back verbally. 'Thanks Jean!' I shot back at her. 'Thanks a lot! Out of everyone involved in this fiasco – the adoption team, children's services and the foster agency – it's you that has made me feel worst! Thanks a bunch.'

David was very upset by my obvious distress. In my emotional state of mind I kept thinking that all he really cared about was the financial aspect and the very real possibility that we could be struck off as foster carers. But he spoke up for me, saying that I was a brilliant mum and if loving a child too much was a crime, then that was all I was guilty of. An extremely taken aback Jean was busily trying to make amends, but I was past caring. Carla also tried to calm the situation by telling us that we could, of course, seek legal advice. I tried to compose myself again and took some pleasure in informing them both that I already had an appointment arranged and would be meeting my solicitor that very afternoon.

That brought the meeting to quite an abrupt end. To her credit, Carla apologised profusely for the turn of events and I, in turn, told her that I knew it was not of her doing and did not hold it against her in any way. Jean, on the other hand, I found hard to forgive. I blatantly ignored her offered apology and left it to David to see her out of the house. I was also – very unfairly – finding it quite difficult to be pleasant to David; I still believed he was not 100 per cent committed to adopting Dale.

5

Being turned down

On Thursday May 5th 2005, David, the children and I arrived at the solicitors' and were directed upstairs to Lindsay Parks's small office. It was quite an achievement for us all to fit into the small room, which was filled to overflowing with lever arch files and other paperwork. Ms Parks was an attractive woman with a capable appearance, and she made me feel at ease from the start. She chatted with Cate and Dale for a few moments before asking us to outline our problem. I began to explain what had taken place up to that point. I had prepared myself by making some notes with a timeline beginning with Dale's arrival up to the present day. I handed it to Lindsay to read. This is what I had written:

July 28th 2004
Dale placed with us for six months maximum

February 11th 2005
A new social worker, Carla, assigned to Dale's case. She was pleasant and friendly. February came and went and Dale remained with us.

April 2005

After careful thought and discussions with my whole family, I decided to approach social services in order to discover what their views were on carers adopting the children they had been fostering. Their initial reaction was very positive: Dale's social worker said, 'How marvellous! You are wonderful.' Encouraged, I took her advice and wrote a letter to the local authority adoption team.

April 15th

I received a letter with an unexpectedly negative response. I telephoned our independent fostering agency in order to seek advice. Our current link worker, Jean, told me that as a fostering agency they could not be seen to support our decision. They would support us "emotionally" and we could write a second letter to the adoption team to appeal against their decision. Letter written and posted on Monday 18th 2005. Letter as follows:

> *Thank you for your letter dated April 12th regarding our request to be considered as adoptive parents for our foster son, Dale. Whilst we accept that we have only been caring for him as foster parents and can appreciate your point that you already have adopters approved, we respectfully ask that you reconsider and allow us to be assessed as permanent parents for Dale based on these facts: He has been in our care since July 2004 and has come to be an important part of our family. Not only do we love him as our own son, but after nearly a year Dale is firmly attached to us and would suffer if he were to be placed elsewhere. Our two daughters have also bonded with him and would be bereft if he was taken from us. It is with this in mind that I appeal against your decision*

*and exercise my right to be assessed as potential
adopters for Dale.*

*Yours sincerely
Helen Jayne*

April 26th
Reply received after approximately two weeks, telling me
that the contents of my letter had been noted and that they
would write back in due course.

April 28th
Jean visited and told David and me that she had been asked
to attend a meeting next day to discuss our case. We were
not invited.

April 29th
Jean visited again to inform us that the meeting had
resulted in the decision to remove Dale from us as soon as
possible. Children's services felt that we had broken our
contract with them and that we would be unable to cope
emotionally with moving Dale on to an adoptive family.
My husband and I deny this strongly. We are committed to
our job – including moving Dale on if that were absolutely
necessary, but we believe it is not in Dale's best interests to
do so.

May 5th
Carla and Jean visited our home. Carla informed us that
social services would identify a new foster home for Dale as
a matter of urgency.

Current situation
Our whole family is distressed by this turn of events. We
feel that decisions are being made, not with Dale's best
interests at heart but in order to prevent us having him in

our care for a full year, thus gaining some legal rights and, as such, an advantage. Whoever actually made this decision is unlikely to know Dale and has probably never met us. They merely intend to move him on, and then to hand him over to adopters without a thought for the chaos they are leaving behind. How can they choose the best life for this little boy if they are not prepared to examine all the options that are available for him?

* * *

Lindsay put the paper down, nodding her head. David then began to talk about our situation and I realised that, whatever he actually felt about my wish to adopt Dale, he was intent on supporting me. I smiled gratefully at him as he explained to Lindsay that while he had not had the same opportunity to bond with Dale, he intended to fight to the bitter end to keep him. Lindsay jotted down some notes before telling us what she felt was the best way forward. She said that we could sit tight and wait to see what the local authority did next. Then if they moved Dale to another foster family, we could decide whether to make an adoption application. Alternatively, we could ask the court for an injunction to prevent social services removing Dale from our care while they assessed us as adopters. We instantly dismissed the first option. It would be bad enough for Dale to have to move at all, but it would be even more confusing and disruptive for him to be moved more than once.

'Well then, we should apply for an injunction whilst we fight to get you approved as adopters.'

We leaned forward to listen more closely.

'This is not a guarantee however. We may not be able to lodge the injunction in time to stop them removing Dale from you. Also, remember it can be quite costly to fight this sort of case. How will you pay for it?'

'Will we be entitled to legal aid?' I asked hopefully. 'We

are on quite a low income from fostering, and now the fish shop has been sold it is only the one income so I am sure we would qualify for some help'.

Lindsay shook her head regretfully. 'No, unfortunately you won't. Reading your brief I can see you own a holiday home. That alone will prevent you being eligible for legal aid. You would be expected to sell that first and use the proceeds to fund your case.'

I felt crushed. I also began to understand the implications of fighting to keep Dale and what it could mean to us as a family.

'What sort of cost are we looking at?' David asked evenly.

'To set the wheels in motion we are talking somewhere in the region of £500–£1,000, depending on whether we need to take counsel's advice,' Lindsay said. She went on to explain that although she dealt in family law, adoption was a complicated matter that might well need her to consult with a barrister. This would increase the cost further as their hourly rates were more than a solicitor would charge.

'It is a lot of money,' I said, wondering how we were going to realistically fund this crusade, 'but £1,000 can't be the reason for not at least trying to keep Dale in our family.'

David agreed but looked somewhat hopeless.

'Why don't you go home, have a chat and give me a ring tomorrow when you have decided which way to proceed?' suggested Lindsay. She shook our hands and smiled encouragingly. I felt she was on our side and that gave me enough hope to go on.

Nevertheless, we left the office feeling downhearted. David was very concerned that we would jeopardise Jordan and Cate's future by sinking funds into what could be a futile attempt to adopt Dale. I could see what he meant but I was reluctant to give up so easily.

'£1,000 will not bankrupt us surely?'

'No,' he agreed, 'but what if the costs rise even further?'

He had a point, and I was struggling with that possibility myself, but still could not bear the thought of letting Dale go without a fight.

'I don't know,' I admitted, 'but I think we should cross that bridge when we come to it.'

I called my parents as soon as we reached home and gave them the facts as we had them from Lindsay. My mum threw a lifeline.

'Me and your dad will give you the £1,000.' she told me.

'We can't accept that from you Mum' I replied. 'This is our fight not yours.'

'It doesn't matter,' insisted my mother, 'we are giving you the money as a gift and it is up to you how you spend it.'

When I told David about my parents' offer, he was not keen to accept the money – he said it was embarrassing and that we should not expect other people to pay for our whims. That was the deciding factor for me. I did not view keeping Dale as a whim and so phoned Lindsay to tell her we wanted to lodge an injunction with the court at the earliest opportunity. She said she would start to get the paperwork in order and we arranged another appointment for the following Tuesday, the 10th of May. This seemed like an eternity away to me in my desperation not to allow Dale to be removed from us. I called my mother back and asked if we could spend the next few days in her house where I was hopeful that no-one would visit in order to take Dale away. Of course she agreed, and the week passed without problems, although it was, at times, quite tricky to cope with the stress. I appreciated my parents, who tried to ensure that our days were spent as normally as possible, so that neither Cate nor Dale sensed anything was amiss. I also made myself a promise that I would not take my underlying fears about losing Dale out on David, as I could understand his point of view and realised that I had not been fair in blaming him for not fighting hard enough for our foster son. We began to talk more openly about what was happening and things became easier between us than they had been in a while.

May 10th arrived and I went to Lindsay's office alone while David watched the children at home. We had both agreed it would be better if I was able to concentrate on what the solicitor said without the children distracting me. However, so fearful was I that someone from the local authority would arrive and take Dale away while I was out of the house, that I made David promise that he would not open the door to anyone unknown to him in my absence.

Lindsay was efficient and to the point. She wanted to take counsel's advice and that would be another £800. I told her to go ahead and she made a phone call to request the information she was looking for. We then discussed our fostering history, I provided some answers to her questions, and she made a few more notes. I had been wondering whether it would help our case if I wrote to our MP and other influential people for help. Lindsay felt that it would not hurt our case at all. I was pleased, as this could channel my energy into doing something useful instead of feeling so helpless. So another appointment was made for the following week and I left the office. The stress of the situation was beginning to tell. There did not seem to be any real progress and I was still terrified that social workers would arrive at any moment to collect Dale. I leant against the wall outside the solicitors' office and rang my mother from the mobile phone. When she answered, I tried to explain what Lindsay had said but instead I began to cry. Mum spoke to me quietly and sensibly about not giving up and I forced myself to be more composed. I didn't want to go home immediately because I didn't want David or the children to see I had been upset, so I sat in the car for a while until my red eyes were less noticeable. The days that followed were a mixture of anxiety and delight. Cate and Dale were so funny to watch. They played together wonderfully, loving each other's company and learning new things almost constantly. Our other foster son was still keeping us on our toes as he continued mixing with a group of young people who were well known for getting into minor trouble with the police. In a way, this caused a helpful distraction as David and I tried to fill his time with activities that interested him as a means of keeping him away from his crowd. He enjoyed computers so we bought him a PC for his bedroom. He seemed to like that, and for a while things ran smoothly as we waited to see what the authority's next move would be regarding Dale.

I also kept myself occupied with writing to people who I thought might be sympathetic to our cause. These included the Children's Commissioner for Wales, our Member of Parliament and the Corporate Director of Social Services. I also made numerous telephone calls to adoption agencies and children's charities across the country asking for any help and advice they could give. In addition to all this activity, I arranged a meeting with a representative of another independent fostering agency as my resentment towards our organisation and towards Jean, in particular, was building and I felt I could no longer work as a carer for them. David too thought that it might be best to move on to pastures new, and so we met with a man named Peter who worked for another independent agency called TACT. He was an extremely affable man who listened sympathetically as we explained our situation. His advice was to attend the next three-day course at TACT headquarters in preparation for joining them, and then to wait and see what transpired with Dale. He wanted to be certain that by changing fostering agencies at this point, we would not jeopardise Dale's position. This made complete sense to us and we agreed to attend the course in a few weeks time. Keeping ourselves busy in this way lowered our state of anxiety, and each day that passed by without social services arriving to take Dale away, gave us more confidence that things just might work out.

On May 17th I was once again sitting opposite Lindsay. She had a large file in front of her with information she had gathered for our case. She began to read out sections she had highlighted:

> 'The court or adoption agency must have regard to the following matters (amongst others):
> (a) the child's ascertainable wishes and feelings regarding the decision (considered in the light of the child's age and understanding),
> (b) the child's particular needs,
> (c) the likely effect on the child (throughout his life) of having ceased to be a member of the original family and become an adopted person,
> (d) the child's age, sex, background and any of the child's characteristics which the court or agency considers relevant,
> (e) any harm (within the meaning of the Children Act 1989) which the child has suffered or is at risk of suffering,
> (f) the relationship which the child has with relatives, and with any other person in relation to whom the court or agency consider the relationship to be relevant, including:
> (i) the likelihood of any such relationship continuing and the value to the child of its doing so,
> (ii) the ability and willingness of any of the child's relatives, or of any such person, to provide the child with a secure environment in which the child can develop, and otherwise to meet the child's needs,
> (iii) the wishes and feelings of any of the child's relatives, or of any such person, regarding the child.

Then she took another sheet of paper and showed me what was written on it.

It said: *'There is a very strong case indeed for believing that prolonged separation of a child from its mother (or mother substitute) during the first five years of life stands foremost among the causes of delinquent character development.'*

I felt triumphant!

'I knew it,' I said, 'if they take him from us now it could ruin his life. He could become a little yob and end up in prison!'

'Let's not get too dramatic,' Lindsay smiled, 'but all this information will go towards making our case in court, should it come to that.'

I tried not to become too excited but suddenly I felt more positive. 'What is the next move?' I asked.

'Now we need to file the injunction with the court'.

I listened carefully to her instructions. Lindsay would complete the necessary paperwork and I was to take it in person to the court and lodge it there the next day. It seemed simple enough. I said goodbye to Lindsay and agreed to return the next morning, Wednesday 18th May, in order to collect and sign the forms.

Next morning, my mother waited outside the solicitor's office whilst I went in to sign the documents. Following the short drive to the city centre, I ran into the court house and waited in a queue for twenty minutes before it was my turn to be seen. With a smile of relief I handed the envelope to the clerk. She opened it and scanned the paperwork.

'I can't accept this from you,' she told me with a frown.

'Why not?' I asked, taken aback. 'It has been filled in correctly and signed hasn't it?'

'It has,' she explained patiently, 'but there are some documents missing I'm afraid.'

'What other documents do you need?' My nerves were jangling and I was becoming flustered.

'I'll need the child's birth certificate and your marriage

certificate. We cannot process this until the court has those documents.'

'I can get my marriage certificate easily but I don't have Dale's birth certificate because he is my foster son not my biological child,' I explained.

'Then you need to apply for his birth certificate and come back when you have it.' She was adamant.

I was close to tears now. All my optimism was ebbing away as the task in hand got more and more complicated. I tried to explain what was going on.

'You see, I am trying to adopt this little boy and social services don't want me to for some reason so I can't imagine them simply handing his birth certificate over to me if I ask.' I was gibbering in my anxiety.

'That won't be a problem at all,' said the clerk kindly, 'just go to the register office and ask them to get you a copy of his original birth certificate. I think it costs about £7.00 if I remember correctly.'

Disbelievingly, I left the court building and Mum and I drove to the nearest register office and went inside. I made my request and was staggered but very grateful at how little information the officials required from me in order to issue a copy of Dale's birth certificate. They merely asked for his date and place of birth along with his biological mother's name. I explained our predicament and they agreed to rush my application through as quickly as they could, although it would not be ready before Friday morning whatever happened.

On the Friday I found myself back at the register office and was handed a copy of the certificate as promised. With that and my marriage certificate in hand, I made my way back to the court and eventually stood before the same clerk I had seen a few days earlier. I handed over the paperwork. She frowned and shook her head again.

'I am so sorry but this marriage certificate is no good,' she said, 'because it is in Spanish and we need a translation before the court will accept it.'

I could not believe so much could go wrong and cause such delay. Time was of the essence if we were to keep Dale. Once more, I returned to the car. Mum had a brainwave and suggested we try the university to get the document translated. We drove there immediately and were directed to the department responsible for translations.

'Yes we can translate it easily. Can you come back next Wednesday?'

Again I described the situation and to my relief the girl made a call and explained the urgency. The voice at the other end agreed to have the document translated by the following Monday morning. We were thankful, but once again we had to return home with mission unaccomplished.

However, the next Monday saw me armed with everything needed to file the paperwork, and this time the whole thing ran like clockwork. After paying the fee, I returned home feeling happier than I had for a long time.

Now the papers were in court, I had a false sense of security that all would be well. The reason I say false is that, after a week had passed and I had not heard anything, I rang the court to find out what was happening. I was then informed that the file had not gone before the Judge yet, and it was not scheduled to do so for at least another week. No amount of pleading or trying to explain what we were going through would move the administrator as he kept reiterating that everyone's case was equally important. With the threat of Dale being taken away, I had no inclination to see his point of view.

On the afternoon of the 10th of June, Jean called at the house. I was alone with the children and I reluctantly opened the door to her. In the back of my mind I wondered whether the local authority would use her to get into my home in order to take Dale away. My worries were unfounded. Jean wanted to keep me updated on what was going on. She had spoken with Carla that morning, and she did not like the fact that we were being kept in the dark for such a long period. That made me feel a little better about her, and we sat down at the table for a cup of tea.

'Carla says that no decision has been taken on Dale yet,' Jean said.

'What does that mean? I asked. 'I understood the decision to remove him had already been made.'

'Well, it seems that the director did not agree with that decision and didn't believe it was in Dale's best interests!'

A lifeline! One tiny bit of common sense at last. I tried not to get too excited.

'So what do you think that means for Dale now Jean?' I asked.

'To be honest, I don't know. However, I think it is good that there seems to be some reconsidering going on, although obviously I don't know what the ultimate decision will be.'

I felt elated that there seemed to be a chance – however slim – and no amount of cautioning from Jean or anyone else could put a dampener on my spirits that day. When David came home, he was so pleased to hear the news and to see me cheerful that we all got into the car and drove to the coast. We spent one of the happiest days in a long time, just walking along the beach and playing ball on the sands. The children had so much fun and the experience made David and me realise that, during our struggle to hold on to Dale, we had not really taken the time to enjoy the children as we should have. Sitting on the dunes later, tucking into a huge bag of chips with the tang of sea air all around us, David and I promised each other that we would always try to remember what was important and meaningful in our lives and not allow outside pressures to destroy that. Later, as I watched both children fast asleep in the back of the jeep on our way home, I realised just how lucky I was to have so much. Now I was more determined than ever to hold on to it.

On Tuesday June 14th, two letters arrived. One was a letter from the court asking us to attend a hearing on the 23rd of the month. The other was a request to attend a pre-adoption medical for Dale at the local hospital. I wasn't sure how to respond to the second letter. I had taken other children for these appointments in the past, usually during the lead up to a permanent family being identified for them. I was worried. Was it a warning that Dale's adoption placement was imminent, or was it just a standard letter, innocently sent? I was unsure, so I phoned Jean and asked her. She told me that it was probably just procedure and that I should not read too much into it. She also reminded me that as the papers had now been filed in court, the local authority could not remove Dale for the time being, so I should try not to worry as much. Somewhat reassured, I tried to do what she suggested. I had begun receiving replies to the various letters I had sent and they were heartening. I felt that David and I were beginning to gather support from some quite influential people, and this gave me hope that things might yet work out just fine.

6

The fightback begins

On June 15th at 10am, Mum and I were waiting to meet with my local MP. I was quite hopeful that he would look at the situation with some sympathy as I had already met him once or twice before and felt he was a very kind and compassionate man. We did not have long to wait before we were called into his office where I quickly launched into details of what was going on. He made some notes, asked me various questions and listened sympathetically as I explained how we felt about Dale. He readily agreed that he would be happy to help us in our fight for Dale but thought we should wait to see what happened at the first court hearing before he began making waves. Glad that someone with some influence was willing to help, I agreed to his suggestion and left his office, relieved that someone like an MP appeared to be on our side.

I awoke on the morning of Thursday the 23rd of June with a churning stomach brought on by nervous anticipation as to what we could expect from our first day in court. The hearing was scheduled for 11am and my mother was looking after both children so that David and I could attend together. Before I left the house, I picked up

Dale and held him close. Soon he was squirming to be put back down again but I held on as long as I could. My underlying fear was that the judge would side with the local authority and rule against him remaining with us and I would have to return home knowing that we had only a short time before we would be forced to hand him over to another carer. It was a horrible feeling.

During the drive to the county court, I could hardly speak for nerves and my inside was in knots. As we walked through the doors of the building, I was shaking and although I tried hard to compose myself, it was impossible. David seemed calmer though, he was holding my hand in his and squeezed it hard as we approached the reception desk. He enquired where we should go and we were directed up two floors where we found some vacant seats and, with some relief, noticed a friendly face. It was Lindsay Parks's legal executive, Phillip Wayne, who was to act on our behalf, and was already waiting for us in the upstairs lobby. He explained what we should expect in the courtroom. I began to feel slightly better as his matter of fact manner helped calm my nerves.

Mr Wayne moved away to prepare some paperwork and I noticed Dale's social worker was also in the lobby accompanied by a woman I did not know. With a smile and a wave Carla got to her feet and greeted us before introducing the other woman as her team leader. Her smile was less forthcoming but I did observe that she seemed as nervous as me, so I forced myself to talk normally about Dale and how well he was doing. I could tell that Carla's boss was fairly uncomfortable with the proceedings and it helped that I was not alone in feeling out of my depth with the whole situation. The woman moved away as hurriedly as she could without appearing rude and began to speak with the local authority's legal representative.

We were then joined by Dale's guardian, Caroline. I hadn't seen her for some time but she was as friendly as ever and we chatted a little bit about Dale and the current circumstances. Then, a concealed loud speaker boomed into life and we were directed into courtroom number five. Phillip Wayne, Caroline, David and I sat on one side of the impressive oak table that dominated the room; the representatives for the local authority sat opposite us. We all rose to our feet as the presiding judge entered the court. Judge T asked us all to introduce ourselves and state our interest in the proceedings whilst he made some notes. He listened attentively as both sides outlined their position. Giving nothing away, he questioned David and me for a short time and listened carefully as we explained our predicament. Then he spoke with Carla's team leader mainly, who appeared to be in worse shape than me. Her hands were shaking and she sometimes stuttered her responses. I felt a stab of sympathy as I could identify with her.

'Has the authority been happy with the care Dale has received from the foster parents during his time with them?'

'Yes.' Her reply was truthful.

'Have any birth family members come forward to care for this little boy?'

'No. There are no suitable family members available. Some relatives of Dale's mother did make an initial enquiry but they were not deemed suitable, and anyway they did not follow it up.'

The judge nodded solemnly.

'Do you have other adopters in mind for the child?'

Once again the reply was, 'No your Honour. The authority has yet to identify any adoptive parents for Dale.'

'The child has been with Helen and David for about a year?' he questioned.

'Yes, your Honour.' This time the reply sounded subdued.

'I don't see a problem then.' Judge T sounded slightly exasperated.

Although I now felt sorry for the woman undergoing the interrogation, especially as she appeared unaccustomed to this kind of experience, relief shot through me and I found my eyes filling up with tears.

'Why has there been such a delay in placing this child for adoption anyway?' Judge T asked the question that I had been wondering myself.

Carla's boss swallowed audibly as she prepared her answer.

'Well, there have been some unavoidable delays,' she began in a quiet voice, 'namely the fact that Dale's original social worker, Hannah, left us unexpectedly. Unfortunately, Hannah had not completed the necessary paperwork and Carla will now need to be responsible for it instead.'

'Mmm, I see.' Judge T sounded less than convinced.

He then turned his attention to Dale's children's guardian.

'Do you see any problems with Dale's care during his time with the carers?'

'None at all. Dale is a happy little boy who has been embraced by both Helen and David's families. He has thrived under their care.' Caroline replied and I smiled gratefully at her.

'Very well. I am adjourning this hearing to enable the authority to arrange to have Dale's current foster parents assessed as prospective adoptive parents. We will convene once more on August 5th.'

My heart began pounding faster. After all the worry of the last few months and all the panic that Dale would be taken from us, the judge had just allayed all my fears with one simple sentence. I was ecstatic and even David was grinning from ear to ear.

Judge T got to his feet and we all followed his example. Then, unexpectedly he turned to David and me.

'How is the little chap doing anyway?' He asked us with a twinkle in his eye.

'Wonderfully, thank you.'

'That's very good to hear.' Seemingly satisfied, he nodded cordially to us all and left the courtroom.

Delighted and encouraged by what had taken place that day we made our way back to the foyer. Carla and her manager walked by and I waved goodbye. Carla looked back over her shoulder and winked at me – I laughed, grateful for her support. That day we had definitely achieved what we set out to get – an even playing field and the chance to be assessed like any other prospective adopter. It was a good result for us.

Feeling better than we had for a long time, we made our way back home where my mother was waiting anxiously for the news. Then we spent an hour ringing around family members to tell them what had happened that day in court.

Things began to get much easier. We no longer had the fear of Dale being removed from us with little or no warning, and for me at least, it was like a weight had been lifted from my shoulders. Now I felt we could move forward and return to some form of normality. I felt happier and more confident that things would work out in our favour. I decided to telephone our MP and the other parties who had shown support for us and who had agreed to help us, in order to make them all aware of our current situation. I spoke with our MP's secretary, who assured me she would pass my message on. Within two days of that call I received this letter:

> *Dear Mrs Jayne*
> *Thank you for keeping me updated of your progress regarding your application to adopt Dale. I am pleased to learn that the injunction preventing your foster son from being removed from your care has been granted by the courts and you are now in a much stronger position. I understand that you will now be assessed as adoptive parents for this little boy. At this point I think my*

> *intervention is unnecessary but please keep me up to
> date with events and should you need my help I will be
> happy to provide it.*
>
> *Yours sincerely*

I was happy to know that even though it appeared things
were going my way, there were still some influential people
I could fall back on in if we hit any further problems.

At the beginning of July, we were notified that we were
welcome to attend the new independent agency's training
course in our local area. It was a three-day course, and we
knew that a number of other foster carers who were slightly
discontented with our organisation were also attending. We
had made arrangements to car share with them and spent
the following three days in a church hall, becoming familiar
with what would be expected of us if we moved from one
fostering organisation to another.

The trainers who were in charge of the "Preparation to
Foster" course were extremely helpful and very
sympathetic about our situation. They told us that if we
had fostered for them, we would have stood a better chance
of adopting Dale, without any complications, as they are
also an adoption agency. They suggested numerous ways
forward and gave us some contact numbers of people and
organisations who might be able to help us. In addition,
some of the other people attending the course had lots of
good advice and encouragement for us. I felt extremely
positive as we said our goodbyes at the end, but I also felt
somewhat disloyal to our own agency as I was very fond of
lots of the staff and carers who worked in it. It would be
hard to leave, and although I continued to harbour feelings
that we had been let down, we decided to stay with them.

A couple of weeks passed by before any more
correspondence came from the authority. However, on July
12th we received the following letter from County Hall:

I write in reply to your letter dated 18/04/05, and am sorry that you did not receive a reply more quickly.

The purpose of Dale's placement with you on 28/07/04 was for him to be cared for in a fostering placement prior to a planned placement with potential adoptive parents. This was consistent with the Local Authority's Care Plan for Dale, which was accepted by the Court when it granted the Authority's application for a Care Order. Unfortunately there has been a delay in the Local Authority implementing this plan and this has resulted in Dale being with you for longer than either you or we anticipated.

I understand that this matter was considered by the Court in the context of the care proceedings in respect of Dale and that a way forward has now been established. Children's Services will meet with yourselves and representatives of your fostering agency to discuss how the assessment of your application will proceed. I have asked the Operational Manager to make the arrangements for the meeting, which will include a suitable Senior Social Worker/Manager who has not previously been involved in decision making in respect of Dale and who has expertise in permanence planning for children. I'm sure you will understand that while there are some similarities there are also significant differences between adoption and fostering and that we cannot assume that people who are assessed as being suitable to foster will be suitable as adoptive parents and the Council's Adoption Service will allocate a social worker to undertake an assessment of your application.

We are grateful to you for the care you have given to Dale during such a significant period of his life and, like you, want to ensure that decisions for his future are made in his best interest.

We would wish to keep disruption for Dale to a minimum and hope that, should the Local Authority decide, after considering your application, that it cannot be approved, you will be able to understand the reasons, although we appreciate that such an outcome would be disappointing for you. The reasons for the decision, whatever it may be, will be shared with you.

Yours sincerely
Chief Children's Services Officer

I instantly bristled when I read the letter. To me it sounded as though the Chief Children's Officer had already made a decision and would do her utmost to find a reason not to approve us as prospective adopters. I said as much to David but he was more confident.

'Don't be silly. What could she find out about us that would prevent us being adopters?' He asked reasonably.

'I don't know,' I admitted, 'but the tone of the letter sounds negative to me and I'm certain we are not flavour of the month with children's services right now.'

'Maybe not,' he conceded 'but they will have a hard job making us look like unsuitable parents for Dale when you have done such a good job so far.'

Whatever his feelings may have been about me wanting to adopt Dale when I first touched on the subject, David was 100 per cent behind me now and I really appreciated his words and belief in me.

The days dragged by. Two weeks after the first hearing, we were back in court and sitting before Judge T to review progress, but no progress had been made. On this occasion, our solicitor suggested we had no need of her Legal Executive's services as things seemed to be going our way. So, with some trepidation, we awaited the judge's comments. There was no need to worry. If anything, he was annoyed with children's services for failing to set the ball in motion. They had not yet appointed a social worker to assess us and the judge could see no reason for the delay. He directed the local authority to organise our assessment as quickly as possible or he would insist that the Chief Children's Officer was brought before him, along with the Director, to explain the hold-up. Once more, David and I left the court very pleased with the way things were going.

The month of August brought some more changes to our lives. Our eldest foster son, Nathan, was moved on to another placement some distance away in an attempt to separate him from the crowd he was mixing with. We were all sad to see him go, as regardless of some of the mischief he had got up to, he was a loving boy who had bonded well with the children and in particular with Dale. In fact, we noticed that Dale was quite subdued after Nathan's departure and we wondered how best to deal with it. We needn't have worried too much however. At about 7pm that very evening there was a knock on our door. It was Nathan. We quickly learnt that he had run away from the social worker who had collected him and now he was hungry. Sitting down to an enormous sandwich, he told us that it had finally been agreed that he could move in with his cousin, who lived locally, if he promised to keep out of trouble. He told us that he would keep in touch with us and visit regularly. We were happy with that as it meant continuity for all the children involved.

September arrived and, as planned, we left Britain to spend our two-week holiday in Florida. The children were really excited about going and on this occasion we had a wonderful, carefree time. All thoughts and worries about Dale's adoption were put aside whilst we enjoyed a relaxed and cheerful break in the sunshine. We took the children to visit some of the Disney parks and they absolutely loved the experience. We spent hours in our swimming pool and Jordan shopped for anything designer she could get her hands on in the malls. We visited doughnut shops and ice cream parlours by the dozen and generally unwound after what had been one of the most stressful times I could remember. When we returned home, we felt ready to face just about anything. Cate was now three years old and it was time for her to start nursery at the local school. She had been looking forward to going and settled in quickly. Dale was a bit miserable without his little playmate at first, but he soon grew accustomed to the new routine and we all adapted.

Prospective adopters as well as foster carers have to provide medical reports to show that they are in good enough health to care for a child. David and I had been told that we would need to have a new health check and that the cost would be our responsibility. We had contacted our GP and been given appointments for Wednesday 21st September. We duly arrived at the surgery and I was called in first. It was to prove an interesting experience. The doctor quizzed me briefly about my lifestyle, checked some basic functions such as blood pressure, read through my medical history and noted that on my last visit I had complained of discomfort in one breast. To my surprise he decided to examine my breasts. As I was putting my blouse on again he saw that David's appointment was next and summoned him into the room. He quickly ran through the same questions before checking on David's last visit to the surgery.

'I see you have undergone a hernia operation,' he announced, looking up briefly from David's file.

David agreed that was correct.

'Well, I just examined your wife's breasts so it is only fair that I examine your testicles.'

To my relief he drew the curtain around the bed so I was not party to his scrutiny. When David emerged from behind the curtain, I could not look at him or the doctor for fear of bursting into giggles. When I took out my purse to pay for the medicals, the doctor told us that he was only going to charge a reduced fee for his services because he thought we were to be commended for applying to adopt Dale and being prepared to fight so hard for him.

We thanked him and left the surgery. By the time we reached the car, I was laughing hilariously although David, for some reason, was nowhere near as amused as I was.

Medicals successfully out of the way, we were finally invited to attend an adoption course at a nearby university campus. It was to run for three consecutive weeks on a Saturday morning and was compulsory if we were to be approved as prospective adopters.

Of course we were glad to attend the course and we got the chance to meet lots of different couples in various situations. One woman, a single mum named Sue, who was on the course with her teenage daughter Jenny, was also hoping to adopt her latest foster child – a little girl who was similar in age to Dale. We chatted to Sue about the circumstances leading up to her decision to adopt and were surprised to learn that she had experienced no complications at all with reaching this point. She thought the difference might be the fact that she was a foster carer for the local authority, whilst we were with a private fostering organisation. The atmosphere on the course was fantastic and very positive. We were very pleased to discover that the woman running it had once been a member of staff at our fostering agency and I had attended some of her training courses. She was very encouraging about our chances of success and made us feel that what we were doing was really worthwhile.

During week two of the course, we were told that a guest was going to visit and speak to us about the adoption process, both as an expert in that field and as an adoptive parent. It was the Chief Children's Services Officer herself.

The prospect of meeting the woman who I thought was against us adopting Dale was daunting and I found myself dreading the final day of the course. However, when it arrived and we were introduced to her, she was in no way the tyrant I had imagined. She spoke to our group about her own experiences as an adoptive parent and I found myself liking her. I can't pretend that she was overly friendly towards David and me, but she was not unhelpful or negative in any way, which was an immense relief to us both.

At the end of the three weeks we successfully completed the "Preparation to Adopt" course and it seemed we were progressing well with our plans to make Dale a permanent member of the family. Friends and family alike commented on how much happier we all appeared to be. We were able to get back to a more ordinary lifestyle, doing things that families usually enjoy together. I began taking both Cate and Dale to a local music and dance class for tiny tots and we started swimming at the local leisure centre once again.

I was now expecting a call any day to let me know when we could expect our assessment to begin. Dale's social worker, Carla, eventually rang and confirmed that a family placement worker had been allocated and that she would be in touch shortly. However, more weeks went by and we didn't hear anything, so I contacted the adoption team again to try and find out what the delay was. They told me that the allocated social worker was off sick, and another had been assigned to us. I was to expect her on Monday October 17th at 10am – almost exactly six months since we had applied to adopt and 15 months since Dale had come to live with us.

My fingers were crossed that this woman would be sympathetic to our cause and not try to sabotage our attempts to emerge from the assessment with a glowing report. The whole situation of being initially rejected by social services as adopters for Dale had left me somewhat paranoid and wary. I wanted to remain optimistic about the way things were going but I couldn't help being nervous in case things went wrong again. It was not a good feeling.

7

The assessment

Right on the hour, at 10am on October 17th, Jan James, our assigned family placement worker arrived. Dressed in a tweed suit, she was a formidable looking woman – tall with short, dark hair and a sober expression. My confidence dipped when I opened the door to her. She spoke in clipped tones with a well-to-do accent. Although I had been told that her initial visit was only to fill in some forms and get signatures, she was keen to meet the children and learn about the situation. When the paperwork was in order, we began to chat about more general things and she told me a little bit about herself and her interests, including animals and her involvement with an animal charity. I began to relax a little. Then she began to ask questions about Jordan's health. She said that she thought Jordan was very thin and wondered if she was suffering from anorexia. Taken aback and annoyed, I found myself getting defensive and denying very forcefully that Jordan was suffering from any eating disorder. I told her how Jordan, like many of her friends, was naturally tall and slim, and like lots of teenagers, ate the wrong things.

Then Jan started chatting to Cate about what her likes

and dislikes were, and made the oddest observation about the cereal I had in my cupboard.

'I like to eat real Kellogg's Frosties. I can see your mum has the Asda brand,' she said, smiling at my youngest daughter.

What? Was I to be judged on what brands of food I purchased? I was getting prickly and finding it more and more difficult to seem agreeable. I attempted to steer the conversation on to when our next meeting would be in the hope that it would bring the visit to an end.

I was very glad when she eventually left and not looking forward to the lengthy assessment process before us. I just hoped Jan James would be reasonable and assess us on our parenting capabilities and not let the fact that I bought an Asda branded cereal distort her view of us. I knew that Dale was really settled and happy living with us and he was certainly developing into a clever and contented child. He called me 'Mammy' and David 'Daddy', just as Cate did and he obviously loved Jordan and Cate very much. I was not clear on how the evidence of Dale's attachment to us as a family would be assessed. I assumed Jan would observe us interacting with Dale and, in addition, would speak to other people who knew us. David constantly reassured me, that we were not likely to have any more problems. However, I was also aware that we had "rocked the boat", so to speak, and felt that we might yet experience some opposition. I could not imagine how we would cope if Dale was taken away at this point; I worried about the impact it would have on the whole family. I thought Jordan and Cate would feel they had lost a brother, and on top of having become deeply attached to Dale, I think David was secretly afraid that, should the worst come to the worst, I would sink into a depression, and this in itself would have a devastating impact on all of us.

We were due to meet Jan again on the 8th of November, and until then I had a lot to keep me occupied. We had accepted a new foster placement – a fifteen-year-old girl who had recently made a half-hearted suicide attempt by taking an overdose of her contraceptive pill. Children's services had told us that they believed it was a cry for attention because she was not happy with her current placement. On meeting her though, it quickly became clear that Jenna was desperate to be part of a family. She had only been living with us for four days when she asked me if I would consider adopting her as well as Dale. She showed such a yearning to really belong somewhere that it made both me and David feel extremely compassionate towards her. I sat with her on her bed that evening and we talked for a long time about being brought up in the care system and how it made children and young people feel. She showed me beautiful and stirring poems she had written and my heart went out to her as I realised just how devastating being passed from foster carer to foster carer could be for a child. It made me more determined than ever to adopt Dale, so that he would never feel like this young girl was feeling.

On the positive side, Jenna seemed a natural with children and that had been one of the deciding factors in placing her with us. Our foster agency believed it would be a good distraction for Jenna to live with a family unit that included Cate and Dale. Jenna was certainly marvellous with them both and they in turn adored her. She enjoyed reading to them and playing with them and I felt the whole experience was good for everyone. The only problem was that Jordan did not like Jenna very much; she felt her to be too needy, and Jenna in return seemed to dislike our eldest daughter. Jordan began questioning the other teenage girl's mental state as well as our foster agency's decision to place her with young children when she had attempted suicide. I explained to Jordan that Jenna was not considered a risk to anyone other than herself. I also pointed out that there would never be a situation when we would leave her alone with the children so there could be no real threat. I put Jordan's objections down to natural rivalry between teenage girls and suggested she should try to be more sympathetic and indulgent.

One early November evening at about six, Dale was doing his usual racing car impersonation, running as fast as his little legs would carry him, at top speed through the house. David had already stopped him running twice but Dale was going through an "I don't like the word no" stage. He raced into the lounge for the third time, laughing delightedly at his own defiance. This time he tripped over his own feet, the speed propelling him forward straight toward the television. His head slammed hard against the cabinet which unluckily had a metal handle on the front of it. Dale let out a shrill scream of pain then began sobbing. Scooping him into my arms I ran to get a cold compress which I held against his forehead. When I removed it to take a look I was shocked to see a huge swelling. Jenna, who had followed me into the bathroom, had some words of wisdom for me.

'Oh, social services will take him off you now,' she informed me in a matter of fact tone.

'Don't be so ridiculous,' I snapped back at her, 'any child can have an accident like this. It doesn't mean he will be taken away Jenna.'

'No, maybe not,' she answered, 'but I bet they are looking for any excuse.'

That hit a nerve – mainly because I wondered if she could be right. Really concerned about the size of the lump on Dale's head, I bundled him into my car and set off for the local Accident and Emergency department, leaving David in charge of the girls. At the hospital, Dale was quickly assessed by a doctor who reassured me that the bump was very minor and he was happy to say that there would be no lasting damage. Dale certainly seemed back to normal, playing with every toy in sight and trying to explore all the rooms going off the corridor. Thankfully, after two hours we were on our way back home with very little to show for the experience apart from a fast diminishing lump on Dale's head and a leaflet on head injuries.

As was expected of me, the next morning, with some trepidation, I reported the incident to social services and our fostering agency; both noted what had happened. I also made a point of speaking with Dale's social worker, Carla, who allayed my fears by assuring me that all children had accidents and I was not to worry about it. Even though I had used almost the exact words to Jenna, I felt much better hearing them from Carla.

Jan returned to continue the adoption assessment on November 8th. This time I was determined not to be cowed by her. I felt the legal system was on our side and I was going to present as confident and in control. The meeting did in fact go very smoothly.

Jan was interested to know our views on discipline and whether or not we would ever "hit" Dale. This is a sensitive area for lots of parents and, personally, I don't think a smack to a child's bottom is harmful in any way. I know when my brothers and I were younger that if we did something that was naughty or considered dangerous it often resulted in a short, sharp slap to the rear, usually delivered by my mum. This meant we seldom repeated the offence. I really do not believe that on the rare occasion my brothers and I were actually smacked, it ever harmed us either physically or mentally; I like to think we have grown up as well-balanced, sensible adults. David's parents had a similar philosophy. David could remember being smacked from time to time as a child, but as he said, the experience was more of a constructive thing as it helped teach him right from wrong. We said that we believed in speaking to the children first and foremost. But I could not rule out ever tapping Dale's bottom. I explained that I felt "hitting" a child was something totally different and much more sinister and that I could promise we would never carry out such an offence against him or any other child.

We also talked candidly about our views on issues such as child care, education, religion and how we would deal with the question of adoption when Dale was old enough to understand. We answered as honestly as we could when we said that we believed it was better for him to grow up knowing we had adopted him than suddenly finding out when he was older.

David and I discussed, too, whether or not to change Dale's name. If Dale had been my own child, I would definitely not have chosen that particular name for him. There was a reason for this. When my brother Craig was in secondary school, he was attacked by another pupil who believed wrongly that Craig had cheated in the dinner queue. This young lad was called Dale. Unfortunately, the incident coloured my view of the name as I associated it with returning home from school and seeing my brother lying bruised and battered on the sofa in the living room. On the other hand, David had always liked the name. In the end, I think the deciding factor was that Dale was already nearly two years old and obviously recognised his given name. We were afraid that changing it might cause some problems around identity and we wished the adoption to be as undamaging as possible. With that in mind we agreed to keep his given name.

During Jan's following visit, she asked if next time she could talk to Jordan. I said I was sure Jordan would have no objections. In fact it was quite true that Jordan was prepared to talk about Dale and the adoption, but she insisted that under no circumstances would she discuss her eating habits with Jan. With some apprehension, I pencilled dates in my diary for future meetings and crossed my fingers that our rather outspoken social worker would not irritate or annoy our outspoken daughter.

After Jenna had been living with us for about two months, she received a letter from the foster carers she had lived with on their farm from the age of eleven to fourteen. Jenna had apparently written to them following her overdose attempt and they were responding to that letter. Jenna had told us that when she lived with Diane and John she had called them Mum and Dad, and on the whole they had enjoyed an excellent relationship. However, during an argument Jenna had insisted she hated living in the country because it was boring and quiet and she wanted to live nearer a town with pubs and clubs. So determined had she been that she wanted a different kind of life that Diane and John had involved the social worker, who agreed to find a new placement for her. Jenna had almost immediately regretted her words but pride had not allowed her to back down and subsequently she was moved from her home of four years. This had been one of the reasons for her unhappiness and silly decision to swallow a pack of her contraceptive pills. Now with Diane and John's letter in her hand, Jenna wondered if they would be willing to accept her back.

David telephoned them and explained how Jenna was feeling. John agreed that they would be happy to have Jenna back if it was what she really wanted. Jenna was ecstatic. She begged us to speak to her social worker and try to persuade her to let her go home to Diane and John. We agreed that we would do our best and called social services the next morning to see what could be arranged. Once it was established that all parties were happy for the move to take place, a date was agreed for Jenna to return to the place she called home.

An excited Jenna asked if her friend Toni could come to stay for the weekend prior to her leaving. We had no objection and the two girls arranged an evening out in a nearby town with Jenna's boyfriend, Matthew, and his friend.

When David picked them up later in the evening it was clear they had been drinking alcohol. Jenna, in particular, was behaving strangely and was unsteady on her feet. I persuaded her to go to bed and sleep it off, but only a short time later we could hear a commotion coming from the bedroom the two girls were sharing. We rushed to the room to find Jenna and Toni arguing heatedly and Jenna throwing things around, including her television and hamster's cage. A frightened and crying Toni began to tell us how Jenna had been experimenting with cannabis during their evening out. At that point, Jenna completely lost her temper and began to punch Toni, who tried to hide behind me. David attempted to calm the situation but it was getting more out of control by the minute.

We went downstairs to make some coffee in order to sober Jenna up, but she immediately made a rush toward the kitchen drawer and grabbed the cheese knife. She began to threaten to kill herself. We both appealed to her to drop the knife whilst Toni made a desperate break for the safety of the bathroom. Jenna rushed after her, tripping over the baby gate which separated the kitchen from the hallway. She, the gate and the knife ended up in a heap on the floor. Still, she was on her feet in an instant and managed to barricade herself and Toni into the bathroom.

At this point I phoned the emergency services as I could not know what she would do next and I was terrified for both her and Toni's safety. David reasoned with Jenna and told her that if she would not open the door he would have no choice but to break it down. Thankfully she did open it and threw out the knife, but she continued to keep Toni a prisoner until the police arrived and persuaded her to come out. Toni was understandably upset, and in addition, she had a bruised face where Jenna had punched her. The ambulance crew checked both girls before the police decided to hold Jenna overnight. She was completely hysterical by this time, crying and pleading to be allowed to stay with us. The police refused, and neither were they prepared for me to accompany her to the station. They half carried her down the drive to their van and peace descended on our home once more. Unbelievably, Dale had slept soundly through all the commotion, although Cate woke and cried when she heard Jenna shouting.

Next day, a contrite Jenna was released back into our care with an extremely stern warning. I explained that her social worker would need to be informed and that it could jeopardise Diane and John's decision to accept her back. She was distraught and pleaded with me not to mention the incident. Much as I wished I didn't have to say anything, because the police were involved, the decision to inform social services had already been taken out of my hands. Later that day, I drove a very subdued Toni to catch her bus home before starting to pack Jenna's belongings ready for her journey back to the country the next day, in the hope that it would go ahead. Jordan, who had been staying at my parents' for the weekend, returned home and reminded me somewhat smugly of her views on Jenna's mental state. In truth, maybe she was the most astute of us all.

Fortunately for Jenna, Diane and John agreed she could still come even after they were told about her behaviour during her night out with Toni. She did, however, have to make them a promise that there would be no repeats of the episode. For myself, I was greatly relieved that they had not changed their minds as I was afraid that if she stayed with us she might do something equally dangerous in the future and I wanted to protect Cate and Dale.

Still, it was a tearful farewell, with a very emotional Cate crying and holding on to Jenna's leg and Dale throwing his Winnie the Pooh at her and locking his fingers around the hamster cage in an attempt to stop her taking the creature away (thankfully it had survived being thrown half way across the room). Jenna and David carried the bags down the drive to the waiting car. She kissed and hugged us all, and then she was gone.

The next day, December 6th, Jan returned for her meeting with Jordan. Nervously I sat in the kitchen with a cup of tea while I imagined what was being said in the other room. When Jordan and Jan emerged, I was pleased to see both were smiling. I chatted with Jan who gave nothing away other than to say I should be proud to have such a sensible daughter. After she left, I confess that I grilled Jordan who told me the meeting had been very positive. It had focused on her feelings for Dale and how she thought David and I would cope with being adoptive parents. There had been no mention of anorexia. Before she left that day, Jan had asked me to name two referees who would support our application and asked if she could speak with my parents as they would provide part of our support network. Things seemed to be coming together and whilst I still felt nervous about the situation, with every little hurdle we successfully got over, the momentum was pushing us forward towards our ultimate goal: keeping Dale safe in our family.

My mother and father were first on the list of referees and I anxiously awaited their call on the day Jan was to visit them. My mother sounded upbeat and excited. She said that she had no idea why I was nervous of the woman whom she had found to be straightforward and charming.

'She asked lots of questions about how we felt about your ability to raise Dale as your own,' my mum told me, 'but she was also extremely positive about how she found you both.'

'Good.' I was quite pleased. If my mother liked her then she couldn't be all that bad!

'She thinks Jordan is lovely and very clever,' my mother informed me.

'Did she mention anorexia?' I asked.

'She did say Jordan is very slim, but she also mentioned

that she had seen her eating huge amounts of chocolate so she was not too worried.'

I laughed at that; I knew Jordan could demolish a bar of chocolate in record time.

'I think it's looking good.' My mother sounded confident.

'I hope you are right,' I said.

The next day my mum handed me a copy of the reference she had written for David and me. I read through it.

How long have you known each applicant and in what capacity?

I am Helen Jayne's mother and mother-in-law to David. I have known David for nine years.

How would you describe the personality of each applicant?

Helen is bubbly, witty and interesting. She also has the ability to think through situations calmly which makes her an excellent decision-maker. David is quietly thoughtful but with a sense of fun equal to Helen's. Both parties are amicable, good natured and have strong personalities, the one balancing the other.

Do you believe the applicants are committed to becoming adoptive parents?

Both Helen and David are one hundred per cent committed to becoming adoptive parents. Just as they have given one hundred per cent to their foster children, striving only for the best for them emotionally, socially and academically within each individual's potential, so they would strive for their adoptive child. This is in keeping with their life aims for their blood children. They have an abundance of love to give, the most important factor, but also commitment.

Their adoptive child would become part of an extended family on both sides, who would love and encourage him through all ages and stages of his life. He would know he was loved and this is the greatest gift any child can be given.

What do you consider to be the strengths and weaknesses of each applicant?

Helen's character is fair minded and just. She is an excellent people person with good organisational skills and communicates well with everyone she meets. Her eldest daughter has been supported in her many facets of life and is an "A" level student. Her younger daughter is being nurtured in the same way and will be given equal support in whatever path she may ultimately follow. If Helen has a weakness, then it is to be too "soft" with the children in her care. Allowing them to often take over situations and have their own way in order to prevent them becoming upset.

David's character is equally fair minded and just. He is a skilled craftsman, balancing Helen's academic bent. The children have always had hands-on experience due to his ability. His laid-back, caring nature makes the time the children spend with him enjoyable and valuable. David's weakness, if it can be called that, is that he is a perfectionist. He will sometimes become so involved in a work venture or situation, often forgetting to take the time to look after himself properly in his enthusiasm to complete a job to the standard he considers necessary.

Between the two, any children they are fortunate to have, will be loved and nurtured to their full potential, whether that lies in academic or practical fields. They will be allowed to become their own people with high self-esteem, a valued thing in today's world.

Do you believe the applicants are suitable persons to become adoptive parents for:

One male child, aged 0–3?
For all the reasons written, I can think of no couple more suitable to love and care for a small boy and nurture him into adulthood.

Any other comments you wish to make.
On a final, personal note, Dale is already a much-loved grandchild for us. Although I have been asked for this reference, my husband concurs with everything I have written and signs to that effect.

I was tearful before I got to the end. Thank you so much, Mum and Dad for all your faith in us.

Around this time, we had another pleasant surprise. We discovered that Jan James had requested a reference from our own support worker Jean. During a routine visit, Jean supplied us with a copy of what she had written.

Dear Jan

Re Helen and David Jayne

Thank you for your letter date November 9th 2005 regarding Helen and David's application to adopt Dale.

Helen and David have been approved carers since January 2002 – however, this was as respite carers (subject to the birth of their own child Cate) with them becoming full-time carers on the 18th of November 2002.

Their approval status is one child or two siblings. In total, they have had thirteen placements including Dale. Helen and David have been involved with mother and baby placements, moving a child on to adoption, and respite placements working alongside children whose ages range from babies to teenagers.

Helen and David have always been consistent in working with our agency and the various local authorities in meeting the needs of children placed with them. They have cared for two very needy brothers who had learning difficulties and significant soiling problems. Due to the high level of need that the boys demonstrated, a decision was made to place them in a home where they were the only children. Helen and David ensured the move was as smooth as possible for everyone concerned.

Helen and David have continued to demonstrate with the placements that they have offered to date, an ability to support and promote contact with significant people in the children's lives.

Helen and David's experiences of raising their own children, together with their varied fostering experiences to date, have provided them with an increasing insight into the implications of disrupted early development and the need to work with children according to their individual levels of understanding.

They provide the children in their care with a safe environment in which to live. They follow safe care practices and a safe caring policy is in place. Helen takes responsibility for completing daily logs and monthly reports on the children in placement. Helen and David have support available to them from both sets of parents who are able to act as sitters if required. They have survived very stressful periods and have supported each other by adjusting their fostering to fit in with their family's needs.

Whilst the couple have managed some difficult placements, only one has broken down. This involved a fifteen-year-old boy who was brought back from an out-of-county therapeutic placement to be closer to his family. Helen and David were very fond of the young person and indeed still see him in the locality and spend time talking with him. The placement lasted for four months.

There have been no complaints or allegations made against the carers.

I have always found Helen and David to be accommodating during my visits. They have always acted appropriately at meetings, being both prepared and able to express their views, and when appropriate, the views of the child. The observations I have made during my visits have always been positive. There have always been age-appropriate toys in evidence alongside the necessary safety precautions, which allow children to grow and develop in a safe and secure environment.

I hope the above answers your questions. However, I am always available for further discussion or to provide further information if required.

Yours sincerely
Supervising Social Worker

In one way I was quite surprised to receive such a pleasing reference from Jean. Although I believed our relationship seemed on an even keel once more, I still felt that some awkwardness remained between us, following her initial response to my adoption application. Now I thanked her; I felt ashamed when I thought back to how angry I had been on that day and I was in no doubt that Jean had not forgotten it either. I just appreciated the fact that she had not held it against me when it came to supplying the reference Jan had asked for.

And so another Christmas came and went in a flurry of activity and excitement. Toys filled the house to an almost ridiculous extent and the children's excitement was palpable. In the middle of January 2006, I heard from our other referees, Phil and Jude, who confirmed that their meeting with Jan had taken place. Vanessa and Andrew's followed shortly afterwards. We were aware that our social worker was going away for a break and we were unlikely to hear from her before March. Now there was nothing to do but wait – and we were getting used to that.

8

A bit of a shock

Thursday January 12th saw me before Judge T at the County Court once again. This time I was alone as David had just launched a new business specialising in timber constructions for schools, and as it was a new venture, he was reluctant to take time off at such a critical stage. We both knew that if our adoption application was successful, the payment we currently received for looking after Dale would stop. Because of all the fuss we had caused in our pursuit of Dale, we wondered if the local authority would place children with us again. Even though our own agency had assured us that we would still be offered suitable placements, we felt it was particularly important to put some money aside as a safeguard.

I was not looking forward to this day as I had been told by Dale's guardian that his birth mum, Angela, would be attending the hearing along with her solicitor. Caroline explained that Angela was coming to court to contest the adoption and I was deeply troubled by this. Apparently she wasn't objecting to us, she just didn't want Dale to be adopted. What if the judge was sympathetic to her case? I knew what a reasonable man he was and wondered if maybe he would be willing to give Dale's birth mother another chance. I was afraid that today could be the day we lost Dale if Angela's appeal was successful. Lots of different scenarios were running through my mind and no amount of reassurance from anyone else was making me feel better. I dressed with more care than usual. I felt the urge to appear in complete control and to convince everyone that nobody could do a better job of raising Dale than I could.

On arrival at court, I scrutinised the waiting area carefully, trying to make out the woman who might be claiming Dale today. I had no idea what she looked like, but there were a couple of women who I believed might fit the bill. Both had quite fair, wavy hair, like Dale, and I tried to match up other features. As it turned out, neither of the women were Angela. She did not show up. My overriding feeling was gratitude. I was so tired of fighting.

Everything ran smoothly. I felt relieved when Judge T decided to grant the Freeing Order, which declared:

> *In the matter of the Adoption Act 1976 and in the matter of Dale XXXXXXX (A Child) It is recorded that the child was freed for adoption by Judge T on January 12th 2006.*

We were another step closer to our goal. Before I left the courtroom, the judge checked on the progress of the assessment and enquired after Dale's health. I told him enthusiastically how well Dale was doing and he seemed genuinely pleased.

Outside the courtroom I bumped into Dale's guardian, Caroline. I told her how nervous I had been and how glad I was that Angela had not shown. Caroline looked at me solemnly.

'Imagine how horrible she feels knowing Dale is about to be adopted?'

'It must be awful for her,' I agreed. 'Yet she didn't

bother to come and fight for him today.'

'No she didn't,' Caroline granted. 'But then she hasn't got your advantages Helen. She wouldn't really know where to start in order to fight for him. She has very little education and has got herself mixed up with a bad crowd. She is no longer with Dale's father and she also has a very bad relationship with her own mother so there is not much family support. I feel sorry for the hand she was dealt.'

I felt chastised. I thought about what Caroline was saying and felt an overwhelming sense of sadness for Dale's biological mother. How dreadful to know that any day now you would lose your child for ever, with no chance of going back. I began to feel guilty knowing how much support and love I had around me when Dale's birth mum was so alone.

'Why do you think she didn't come today Caroline? Surely it would have been better for her to at least try and fight for him?'

Caroline shook her head.

'I am pretty sure Angela was advised that whether she contested or not, the judge would grant the Freeing Order. Not many mothers have it in them to simply give their consent to an adoption going ahead and so she probably felt she had to say "no", just to make a statement, but in the end it was easier to do nothing.'

I could actually understand that. Thinking about what Caroline was saying, I realised that I could never simply agree to any child of mine being put up for adoption. With the odds so stacked against her, Angela was obviously in a hopeless situation. There and then I decided to compile a book of photos for Dale's real mum. I ran the idea past Caroline and she agreed that it would be a good thing to do. I decided I would leave the book with children's services so that if Angela ever got in touch with them, it would be there waiting for her. I felt the need to somehow give something back to the woman who, after all, would probably soon lose her son for good.

As I left the court that day, regardless of the fact that I knew we were closer than ever to making Dale a permanent member of our family, I did not feel triumphant. Instead I felt almost unhappy that our success was at such a cost to another person. It was a sobering thought.

The day did not get better. When I got home, it was to find a letter awaiting me from the local hospital with an appointment for an update adoption medical. I scanned the letter and froze as I took in the contents: Dale will require blood tests, as there is a possibility he may have been exposed to a blood-borne virus.

David had just returned home for lunch and I looked at him in horror.

'What does that mean?' I asked. 'The only blood-borne virus I can think of is HIV!'

'I don't know,' replied David, 'but it is certainly something we need to find out about as quickly as possible.'

Feeling worried and confused I rang Jean to ask her if she knew anything about the letter I had received. She was as baffled as I was but she promised to phone Carla and try to get to the bottom of the whole thing and we waited anxiously until she called us back.

'I'm afraid Dale was born with withdrawal symptoms.' Jean told me sombrely. 'His mum was a drug addict and she continued using throughout her pregnancy.'

'Yes, I did read about that in his notes,' I said, 'but the reports we had didn't say anything about the possibility of him being infected with any virus.'

'No, you're right.' Jean replied. 'We don't seem to have any reference to that fact here either.' There was a pause.

'Look Helen, I think we need to get him tested as quickly as possible in order to rule out anything like HIV or hepatitis.'

For a moment I couldn't think straight. I didn't know much about either HIV or hepatitis but I immediately began to worry that if Dale did indeed have any kind of virus, we may inadvertently have exposed Cate or even Jordan to it. Suddenly I felt sick.

I called my parents who were aghast at this new turn of events.

'Good God! Why didn't anyone warn you about this?' Mum asked me angrily.

'I don't know. I suppose they assumed I would have thought of the possibility.'

In all honesty I did actually feel rather stupid for not considering such a frightening scenario when I first accepted the placement, as I had been fully aware of Dale's mum's history. In addition, I had been to numerous training sessions and seminars where similar situations had been discussed. However, it had not really crossed my mind that we could be faced with such a problem ourselves, as I believed we would never be asked to care for a child who might pose a significant danger to our own children.

The possibility of Cate being infected through Dale had entered my mum's mind too and I could tell she was really upset. I tried to put my own fears aside to reassure her.

'Mum, I'm sure he is OK. Look how healthy he looks and he very rarely gets ill even with coughs and colds. That would be one of the symptoms of a low immune system, which I think would go hand in hand with a virus like HIV or hepatitis.'

In reality though, I did not know. I had no idea what this new development could mean for us.

'What will you do if Dale is infected?' Mum asked the question I had been too afraid to think about.

'We will just have to deal with it.'

'But it will affect all your lives, including Jordan and Cate.'

The whole situation was too horrible to contemplate and I really did not want to dwell on what the future might hold for any of us if Dale was either HIV positive or carried the hepatitis virus through his biological mother.

'I just know that I have fought for him this long and I will carry on fighting for him no matter what.'

I could not see any future without Dale, and I knew my parents understood that fact no matter how worried they were.

The next morning, I telephoned Dale's social worker, Carla, and spoke to her in some depth about this new hurdle. She was sympathetic and reassuring, and promised that she would get a hospital appointment sorted out very quickly. She could not explain, however, why we had not been informed of the possible problem when Dale was first placed with us and told me that she would look into it. I appreciated her obvious concern but it did nothing to lift the worry that hung over us like a dark cloud for the next week.

The situation certainly had far-reaching implications. From the moment the information was given to us, we became obsessively overcautious about everything Dale did. We panicked if he fell over in case he cut himself, so frightened were we of him bleeding. We stopped him and Cate swapping bottles, cups and dummies as they always had – just like any other brother and sister. Suddenly the thought of them sharing food and drink or anything else that might allow an exchange of bodily fluids became a huge "no, no" for us. I was a nervous wreck. The happy feeling I had enjoyed since Judge T agreed to us being assessed as adopters for Dale had almost entirely dispersed. I felt that we were being punished in some way for causing such a commotion. On the one hand, I kept telling myself there was no way this gorgeous and happy little boy could be ill, as he looked so robust and healthy. On the other hand, I fretted that he had an incurable illness, which could already have been passed to one or indeed all of us. It was a distressing time.

A few days after receiving the letter, Carla phoned to say she had decided to call a meeting in order to discuss the implications of the information we had received. She would bring a senior manager and I asked Jean to attend.

I felt uneasy about the meeting from the start. I remembered all too well the last time I had sat in my lounge with Carla and Jean and I was anxious that bad feelings could resurface. My fears were justified when Carla's manager, on the defensive, began to speak about Dale and the current situation.

'Surely you understood the implication of caring for a child born with withdrawal symptoms?' she asked.

I was immediately irritated and replied, 'Well, it was never suggested to us that Dale could be carrying a dangerous and highly contagious illness – so no, not really'. 'Yes, but you have a safe caring policy in place surely? With any foster child you would do things like wear gloves if he or she had a cut you were tending to, or that kind of thing?'

Dale toddled into the room at that moment. His hair was falling in little ringlets around his face and his cheeks were rosy. He smiled with delight when he saw new people in the room and ran to me for a cuddle, shyly looking around him. As I hugged him to me tightly, I knew that no matter what we discovered, I would continue to love and care for this little boy just as I did now. As far as I was concerned, he was my child and I intended to protect him and keep him from harm as long as I lived.

I looked straight at Carla's manager.

'Yes we do have a safe caring policy in place. But obviously Cate doesn't have one. How would you expect me to stop these babies who live under the same roof sharing dummies and toys, etc.? No one can watch children twenty-four hours a day – no matter how well intentioned they are. There will always be moments when the children are alone together. Not just here in this house but in any home. How did the authority expect me to stop that happening when they placed a child with me who may have HIV?'

The manager could not hold my gaze and I realised that she had no answer. She stuttered a little and then attempted to steer the conversation away from the awful subject we were discussing.

'Mama cuddle Dale,' said Dale in his sweet baby voice and everyone in the room laughed.

I felt somewhat vindicated because without having been given more precise information at the start of the placement, I really believed we couldn't have assumed or guessed that Dale might pose a risk to us.

The meeting drew to an end and Carla and her manager took their leave. Jean stayed behind for a few moments.

'I agree totally with what you are saying,' she said. 'You had no way of knowing that the authority believed Dale to be at risk of HIV or hepatitis. I will make sure that his hospital appointment is rushed through so that we all know exactly what we are dealing with.'

David and I thanked her but we knew our lives would change unrecognisably if Dale were infected with any kind of transmittable virus. That much was certain. In addition, if he did test positive, the whole family would need to be tested to determine whether or not we too were infected. I was constantly fighting down an urge to panic. I was so afraid and could only pray that our worst fears would not be realised. A week went by and we did not hear from the hospital. I took matters into my own hands and telephoned the paediatrician who had seen Dale for his adoption medical. She confirmed that she was aware of the situation and promised to expedite his appointment. True to her word, she rang me back with a date and a time. Two days later, David and I drove Dale to the hospital and I held him whilst the Doctor took some blood to be analysed. I asked how long we were likely to wait for the results and was told we should know within a week.

The waiting was very hard. David and I kept telling ourselves that Dale would be fine. He had never shown any signs of being unwell, apart from normal problems like teething or colds, and we tried to remain optimistic.

We also tried to talk about what it would mean to us all if Dale was ill but the conversations were too difficult, and I invariably ended up in tears. I think David felt hopeless as this was a situation that he could not take control of, and I was afraid he thought that Cate or Jordan might well be at risk of a dangerous illness through my determination to adopt Dale. That in itself made me feel very guilty. However, I tried my best to remain upbeat because I didn't want Jordan to be afraid of the outcome, or Cate and Dale to pick up on my terrible anxiety. I also didn't want my parents to be more upset than they already were by what was going on, so I kept assuring everybody that I was 100 per cent certain Dale was in the clear. David had decided not to tell his parents, so the problem was never mentioned when they came to our house to see the children.

Eventually, a letter arrived stamped with the hospital frank. I tore it open and scanned the contents. I nearly fainted with relief.

'I am pleased to confirm that the results of Dale's recent blood tests were negative.'

The words swam before my eyes. I phoned David and told him quickly that Dale was OK. Then I called my parents. They were so relieved, and at that point I finally began to cry. Tears of immense gratitude and joy.

9

Facing the panel

With the dark cloud over Dale's health lifted, we all felt that we could begin to enjoy life again. There were lots of things taking up our time now: David's new business was growing, Jordan was studying hard for her "A" level examinations and both younger children needed lots of attention. In addition, as foster carers, we were regularly invited to attend training sessions, support meetings and various other get-togethers involving the fostering agency. January was no exception with our annual appraisal due as well as a LAC (Looked After Children's) review for Dale.

Our appraisal in early January, which always took place in our home, ran smoothly with no major issues being identified. I had worried a little about it as I felt in a way that I had disappointed our fostering agency with my decision to adopt. I felt less comfortable than normal as the meeting began and I was relieved when it finally drew to an end.

Dale's LAC review followed soon after. As usual, David and I travelled to the family centre to meet with the now familiar faces present. Again, I felt somewhat awkward as I sensed that some of the staff probably saw me as a troublemaker after everything that had transpired. However, everyone was extremely professional, and we had the normal discussion about Dale's welfare before the adoption plan was even touched on. I was relieved when the adoption process and what David and I could expect in the coming months was talked about without reference to earlier problems. We were also notified that the reports and paperwork that should have been completed by Dale's original social worker, months before, were now almost finalised and would be ready to be submitted to the court. That was good news and another positive step in the right direction. Nevertheless, once again I was relieved when the meeting was over.

As Dale's second birthday was fast approaching, I thought it would be great fun to celebrate it with a party for family and friends. I busied myself with party preparations, buying cakes and crisps and making jellies and other treats that I knew the children would enjoy. Balloons and banners were put up around the house and I invited guests. David and I wondered what to buy for Dale. On his first birthday, when we believed he would be moving to another adoptive family, we had bought items which could easily move with him, and some that could be keepsakes including a gold St Timothy necklace. Now I wanted to make up for the previous year and buy lots of toys to fill his bedroom. David said he would prefer to put money into a trust fund for Dale. So, in the end we settled on a Little People Train Track and some toy cars, books and teddy bears as well as a lump sum placed in his fund.

The county had been warned to expect snow, and I was concerned that we would have to postpone the celebrations. When the day arrived, the sky did look particularly heavy. I had organised the party for the Sunday closest to Dale's actual birthday. At 2pm guests started to arrive: first my youngest brother and his girlfriend, followed closely by my parents, David's mum and dad and his brother and family. Our neighbour, Vanessa, and her daughter joined us and Jordan's friends came too. Dale's excitement was wonderful to see. He thoroughly enjoyed ripping open the wrapping paper covering his numerous gifts – in fact he seemed more taken with the paper than with what was inside! Dale was laughing and smiling at everyone and delighted by the huge fuss being made of him. But Cate was a little peeved that her brother was getting all the attention. She tried hard to upstage him by dancing and singing and everyone thought her antics were very funny. The atmosphere was light hearted, the snow held off, and it was agreed that the party had been a great idea. I put a totally exhausted but happy Dale and Cate to bed that evening.

March 2006 arrived and we knew that a phone call from Jan James to say her report was complete was imminent. When the call did come, my nerves jangled. I desperately wanted to know that the assessment was favourable and that Jan was recommending us as adopters, but I feared that maybe she would have been influenced by bad feeling toward us because we had forced the local authority to go to court over Dale.

Jan, in her usual no nonsense tone, gave nothing away and told me she would visit on the evening of March 10th to allow David and me to read and sign her report. She also told me that we were scheduled to go before the adoption panel on March 22nd.

A couple of days later, when Jan arrived, I tried to act as composed as possible. It was not easy. I so much needed to know how we had done but was too afraid to ask. All sorts of questions had been running through my mind. Did she consider us good parents? Had we made the grade to be accepted by the adoption panel? David, in his down-to-earth way, made us all a pot of tea and we sat down together at the kitchen table. Cate and Dale, as active and inquisitive as ever, were running back and forth between the lounge and kitchen, where Jordan and my mum were waiting. Jan chatted indulgently to both children, and although I was incredibly anxious to find out what was in her report, it was good to see that she obviously liked the children and that they liked her.

When she transferred her attention to David and me, she smiled and I suddenly thought how compassionate her eyes looked. I was feeling less nervous now and smiled back. She explained that we could read her assessment, and if we were happy with everything it contained, we should sign and date it so she could submit it to the panel. She handed David and me a document each and we both started to read.

The report began with some personal information about us as a family. Jan had asked us both to describe our backgrounds and how we had met. This is what I had written:

> *My name is Helen Jayne and I am 39 years old. I was brought up in the Rhondda Valleys – a place I love very much. I had an extremely happy childhood, living with my parents, two brothers and paternal Grandmother. In 1989 when I was 21 years old my whole family relocated to the Costa del Sol, Spain where we spent an enjoyable six years living on the coast running a water sports business. Due to some financial problems, my family returned home in 1995 and I met David a year later during my first year at University where I studied English. In 2001, David and I married in the Dominican Republic with both our families present.*

> *My daughter Jordan (from an earlier relationship) is now 19 years old and studying for her "A" Levels in English, Law and Religious Education with the intention of going on to University. David and I also have a daughter together, Cate, who was born in 2002.*

In 1997, David and I bought a beautiful four-bedroom detached home. Our house is in a semi-rural position and backs on to the mountain where we can enjoy wonderful walks with our pet Labrador, Fudge. The house itself is extremely spacious and consists of a large lounge, sitting room, dining room and kitchen as well as four bedrooms. David has landscaped the front garden and the rear garden is mainly lawn to allow the children (and dog) to play safely.

My father is a successful businessman who runs a discount store in the Rhondda helped by my oldest brother. My mother is a schoolteacher who absolutely adores her job and who I believe has been inspirational to many young people over the years with her amazing ability to make learning fun.

My previous employment was as an administrator with the health service. In 2001 however, I decided I needed a change and after speaking to David, decided that I would love to look after other children and provide them with opportunities that maybe they would not otherwise get. David and I have been foster carers since January 2002 and I personally find it an enjoyable if challenging career. I have had the opportunity to look after many children over the last couple of years and have thoroughly enjoyed the experience.

I carried on reading what Jan had written and couldn't hide my delight. She had made observations and comments and all of them were positive.

The report dealt with the BAAF course we had attended. It read as follows:

Applicants attended the BAAF course for prospective adopters. There were no concerns and the applicants were seen as experienced carers with insight into the needs of children placed away from their birth family.

It went on to say:

They recognise adoption is different from fostering and identified how those differences might affect their family. They showed lifelong commitment to the child and recognition that adoption is a life-long process, requiring sensitive support through childhood and into adulthood. They were positive about promoting identity and sharing information about the past appropriately and understood the importance of contact, direct and indirect. Although Helen and David had existing knowledge, they participated fully and used the course to develop their understanding. They demonstrated good verbal and written communication skills and evidenced commitment to the child with an emphasis on positive supportive family relationships.'

Helen and David inform me they found the course very useful and enjoyed attending. They learnt a great deal about adoption generally and it gave them much to think about.

Interestingly, one segment of the report shed some light on why we were told we would not be considered as adoptive parents for Dale. Under the title "Existing Foster Carers Wanting to Adopt" was written:

It transpires that Helen and David are not local authority carers and they should have had Dale for three years, not one year as the judge declared, before making an application. It was, however, considered not to be in Dale's best interests to delay the matter further by contesting the legality of the order.

Another section was entitled "Reunification implications for a child being reunited with birth family."

The care plan put to the courts was for adoption of Dale, so there is no plan to continue contact with birth family or to look to rehabilitation.

Helen and David will not need to consider ways of familiarising Dale to a new environment if he is adopted by them, as he will see little change to his life. Although social workers visit now, he is a little too young to realise they are visiting to ensure his well-being. When I have visited, he and Cate try to get me to join in their games, give up for a while, then they try again. They both just see visitors to the family home as distractions from their games. There are many visitors as it is a busy household.

I do not know if the birth parents know that an application to adopt has been made by the present foster carers, but they were aware of the Care Plan for adoption.

From reading the child's file it seems the parents say they do not agree with the plan for adoption but neither parent has attended court for some considerable time. Mother did request family members be assessed to care for Dale and this was done. Dale's maternal grandmother is in poor health and Dale's aunt and partner withdrew their interest in caring for Dale. There has been no contact with extended family for some time.

Dale has two older half-brothers who were adopted together some time ago, and there was little information on Dale's file. The applicants are aware of this and the social worker states that this information will be in Dale's life story work. Helen and David are aware of the organisation "After Adoption" and they will consider seeking advice, guidance and support for Dale as he grows older and looks for information about his half-brothers. They will facilitate any letterbox contact that is required but I understand there is to be no contact with the half-brothers, and the birth parents' future wishes will need to be clarified by the adoption reports to the courts.

Numerous other sections followed until we came to "Assessing Social Worker's Recommendations":

Helen, David, their children and extended family, look upon Dale as a member of their family and care for him as such. He has now been in placement for over 18 months and would not remember any previous carers. He is a happy, sociable little boy, very boisterous and he can be very noisy, but he clearly loves all members of the household. He openly shows them affection and he and Cate are particularly close. I would recommend that it is agreed that Helen and David may adopt the child Dale, as it is in his best interests to remain with the family that he considers his own.

When David and I had finished reading, we were both smiling. Some of the things that Jan had written were very amusing – she had commented on how child-friendly the home was and said that everywhere she looked there were children's toys in sight (something that actually irritates David, as he believes some of the rooms should be for adults to relax in and free from children's clutter).

My initial reaction was of complete relief. The assessment was more positive than I could ever have imagined. I have copies of the report – and even though it might sound "glowing", that is as it is. This woman, who I had been so panicky about, had done us, as a family, proud. The thing that shone through most was how much we all loved Dale. I found myself emotional yet again, knowing that someone else was on our side. To be truthful, until that day, Jan's overall manner had always been so professional and neutral that I had been unable to gauge her real feelings about us. In the event, she had written her appraisal fairly and with no bias whatsoever. It was simply her impartial account of our family life, with contributions from us and our referees and Jan's final recommendation that, in her view, we should indeed become Dale's parents. I wanted to hug her but thought I might embarrass her because of her tendency to keep herself aloof. However, I kept thanking her over and over and saying how grateful I was and David was doing the same. The children picked up on our obvious excitement and the whole atmosphere in the house became almost frenzied as Cate demonstrated her dance technique and Dale showed off with his puppy dog impersonation. Jan remained unruffled by it all and even told us that she had found us a co-operative and loving family. She drew our attention to her comment that she could not locate a room in our home, which did not contain children's toys. We all laughed at the accuracy of her observation, even David.

We then signed and dated her report and after another cup of tea, in what could only be described as a celebratory mood, Jan James popped into the lounge to say goodbye to Jordan and my mum before taking her leave. My mother hugged me and said, 'You see? Nothing to worry about. I told you Jan was alright!'

David rang his parents and shared our good news with them.

Now, all we needed to do was face the adoption panel. Even that seemed less daunting once we knew Jan's assessment was so positive. We even began to look forward to the day when we would sit down and meet the people who would recommend whether or not we were a suitable family for our little Dale.

The time passed quickly and before we knew it, the day we were to meet the panel was upon us. My mum arrived early in the morning so she could get Cate ready for school, allowing David and me to prepare for our important meeting. Dale would remain in the house with Mum until we returned with either good news or bad.

The weather was blustery and when we arrived at County Hall we were buffeted by the chill breeze as we walked across the car park and entered the building. We climbed the winding staircase and sat in the chairs outside the room where a panel of people would decide Dale's future as well as our own. Carla arrived and wished us luck before the door opened and we were ushered in. We sat down a little apprehensively and looked around us. Brief introductions were made and we nodded and smiled at everyone present. I recognised a few people from children's services. Regardless of our newly-found confidence, my heart was hammering in my chest and I could tell by David's face that he was fairly anxious too. The moment had at last arrived when we would discover whether our struggle to keep Dale would finally succeed. As I glanced around the table though, I realised that everyone present just looked ordinary and friendly. There did not appear to be any frowning or distrustful faces. I brought my attention back to the woman who had introduced herself as the Chair; she began to discuss our application. She asked a few questions about Dale in general. She was particularly interested to know why Dale was special. It wasn't difficult for me to tell her.

'When Dale first came to live with us we thought his stay would be short. I tried not to bond too much with him because I knew from past experience how hard it would be to let him go. However, when there was no other family after almost a year, I knew I couldn't part with him. We had grown to love him so much. And not only David and I, but our families also love him. As far as we are concerned, he is Jordan's and Cate's brother and both girls would grieve incredibly if he had to leave us. Our parents love Dale as a grandson. And, more importantly, Dale loves us all as his family. I truly believe he would be unhappy and distressed if he was taken from us, and furthermore, I think it would impact negatively on his development. I know people say children are resilient and can cope with whatever life throws at them but he doesn't need to cope with it. We are here for him, we want him to stay with us and bring him up as our son and we don't want him to find out in the future that he was placed with a loving family who badly wanted him to become their son, but he was uprooted for no real reason and put with other people who may not even care about him like we do. He is so special and clever. He already has a large vocabulary and you would not believe how dexterous he is. The health visitor recently assessed him and he was way ahead in reaching his milestones.'

I was speaking quickly and nervously. I was proud of Dale's achievements and I paused for breath at this point. The Chair, smiling broadly, stopped me by raising her hand.

'We can all see how much you love him,' she said, still smiling. 'When you speak about him your whole face lights up. It is certainly clear to me that he is very dear to you indeed.'

I was moved to hear that someone was acknowledging how we felt about Dale. It was extremely important to me that everyone in the room understood why I had felt the need to fight so hard to keep him. It had never been merely a whim or wanting to be difficult because my request to adopt had been denied, which I sometimes felt was in people's minds. Instead, there was a strong mutual attachment that I could not and did not want to sever.

At last, the people who had the power to make recommendations seemed to understand where I was coming from and that was the most important thing I could ever have achieved.

However, because I felt so overwhelmed to have actually reached this point, I could not have been concentrating fully, because to this day I cannot accurately recall what more was said during that meeting. I vaguely remember other panel members asking us questions, and I assume we gave adequate answers because everybody seemed relaxed and affable. I cannot even clearly recall at which point we were told that our application had been wholeheartedly approved. I do remember thanking everyone profusely and I also remember leaving the room and hugging Carla outside in the rather cramped corridor. After a year spent fighting for Dale, we were finally being accepted as his parents.

10

Our day in court

After we had been approved by panel, I can honestly say that our home seemed like a different place. The whole atmosphere was lighter and we seemed to get on better, with less petty arguments and tensions. I don't think any of us had realised how stressed the whole adoption business had made us, and it was a relief to find ourselves on the other side of a difficult patch and still talking to each other! One morning, as I sat in the kitchen watching Cate and Dale playing together, I felt a lump come to my throat. Cate was "Mammy" and Dale was being her baby. He was so happy to be playing with his big sister and his smiles and chortlings moved me.

'Can this Mammy join in?' I asked.

Cate laughed. 'Yes but you have to be big sister because I am the mammy.'

'OK,' I agreed, 'What do you want me to do Mammy?'

'I want you to take Dale to the shops because I need some bread. Then you have to go and see if the judge will let him stay with us.'

I was completely taken aback. Cate was obviously very aware of what had been going on in the household over the last year even though she was still only three years old. It was astounding.

'Do you think the judge will let Dale stay with us Mammy?'

Cate was suddenly very serious and I took a deep breath before I answered her. 'I think so darling. Dale has been here a long time now so I hope everyone knows that it will be best for him to stay with us.'

Cate seemed satisfied and turned back to Dale and they went on playing.

Her unexpected question had troubled me however. Whilst being so wrapped up in the battle to adopt Dale, I hadn't thought carefully enough about the devastating impact it would have had on Cate, and indeed Jordan, if he were suddenly taken away from us. Most of my focus had been on how Dale would react if he were separated from me and the people he knows and loves. I had thought about him being with strangers and how it would affect him. I had worried about him being scared or confused. I had even imagined scenarios with adopters who mistreated him or that the placement broke down. All these possibilities had upset me and had been the driving force behind my fight to keep Dale with us. Now I was confronted with yet another problem. If we did fail at this last hurdle, I would have allowed Cate and Jordan to bond with Dale for much longer than they would have if he had been moved to another adoptive or foster family earlier in his life. The separation would be even harder on everyone after all this time and it would be all my fault. I could not bear the idea of losing Dale and I could only imagine how much harm I would have done to all three children if the judge ruled against us. It was a frightening prospect and regardless of the positive outcome of panel, I felt afraid again. However, I did not want to dampen the happy mood in the house and decided it was better to keep any fears to myself.

We had one more day in court scheduled for the judge's

final directions on April 10th and regardless of my niggling worries, I did feel more confident than I had in the past. Judge T acknowledged us in the courtroom and asked affably if everyone was happy. David and I said we were. He consulted his notes and asked if everything was now in place for the date to be set for the adoption hearing. Carla's team manager spoke:

'We have identified a slight problem I'm afraid.'

'What is it?' The judge peered over his glasses.

I leaned forward in my seat and David looked and me, puzzled.

'We have had all the police checks back on Helen and David and it has come to our attention that there is a gap in Helen's record. It seems she lived in Spain for a few years and unfortunately our criminal records don't cover offences committed whilst abroad.'

'I see,' the judge consulted his paperwork. 'What can be done about this?'

'I am not sure what is the best way forward,' admitted the team manager.

'Very well.' The judge looked down at his papers again. Then he looked gravely at me.

'Did you commit any offences whilst living abroad?'

The question made me smile even though I was aware that it was a most serious issue.

'No I didn't.' I replied, hoping I sounded like an honest person.

'Well, we could contact the Spanish authorities and ask them to confirm what Helen has said. However, the Spanish people are not known for their propensity to rush are they?'

He looked at me, this time with a twinkle in his eye.

'No they certainly are not!' I agreed emphatically. If there was one thing I had learned during my time in Spain it was that Spanish people were never in a hurry. My father once waited for 18 months for the Spanish authorities to make a decision on whether or not to grant him a licence to run a small business from the port near our home. No amount of phone calls, letters and pleading, or even angry face-to-face confrontations had moved the powers that be. Like most other people who have chosen to make their homes in Spain, we had become very familiar with the word "*mañana*".

'Would you be prepared to swear on the Bible that you have never committed an offence while you were living in Spain?' Judge T asked.

'Yes, of course.' I agreed instantly. I didn't think my nerves would hold out if there were further delays.

'I'll adjust the paperwork and we'll overcome the problem that way then. Does the local authority have any objections?' He looked at Carla and her team manager.

They both shook their heads and smiled. I think they were as happy as we were to bring the episode to a close and draw a line under it all at last.

Within fifteen minutes, I had sworn on my oath that I had never been in any trouble with the police during my years living in Spain. The judge and the local authority seemed satisfied and we were given a date for the adoption to be made final: June 7th 2006. In less than two months Dale would legally be our son. As we left the court for the penultimate time, I was shaking with relief. Jordan and Cate would not need to be separated from Dale after all. They would always remain siblings, and the emotional damage I feared I might have caused the children was something I needn't have worried about after all. Our lives would go an as I had envisaged, as a family of five and not as a family of four.

The time flew by. We knew Judge T would not be at the final hearing and I was a little disappointed as he had been such a huge support throughout the case and I had hoped he would be there at the end. A more senior judge would sign the adoption order. The hearing would give us the chance to bring the family to court and to record the happy event.

Now that I was almost certain Dale would remain with us as a proper and permanent part of the family, I felt more able to plan for him. David and I decided that he would benefit from attending a local nursery school for half a day to give him a chance of meeting other children – especially as Cate was now at nursery herself and he missed her a lot in the day. Dale loved nursery. He was such a sociable little boy and quickly became one of the most popular children in the class. It was fantastic to see how he mixed so well with other children and threw himself into all the games with such enthusiasm. I was so proud to be his mum. It was a good feeling.

One rather sad event took place at this time however. I had done what I had told Dale's guardian, Caroline, I would do and had compiled a book with photographs of Dale, drawings and paintings he had done both at home and in nursery, and some short paragraphs describing his likes and dislikes. I had given it to Caroline who had told me she would lodge it with children's services. Out of the blue I got a call from a social worker named Grace.

'I understand you have left a photo album here for Dale's biological mother.'

The woman sounded peeved and I was puzzled.

'Yes. That's right.' I agreed. 'Is there a problem with that?'

'I'm afraid there is.' She confirmed. 'We don't have any room to keep such things and I have to return it to you.'

'Oh!' I was taken aback to say the least. Here I was thinking I was doing something nice for Dale's mum and it was being thrown back in my face.

'In addition, the photographs are not appropriate at all,' she went on, 'they show him in a playground that could be identified by his mum.'

'I don't think so.' I argued. I had deliberately chosen

photographs that would make it difficult to pinpoint Dale's whereabouts. I knew the photograph Grace was talking about, but it simply showed Dale on a red slide, laughing uproariously as he was sliding down towards me.

'Any number of playgrounds could have had the same equipment,' I insisted.

'Well, nonetheless I have to return it to you,' she told me emphatically. 'I can't post it to you for fear it falls into the wrong hands.'

Good God! I felt like I was involved in espionage of some kind. It seemed ridiculous to me that one small act, of what I thought was kindness, could be turned into such a big and unpleasant deal.

'Fine!' I retorted, knowing I sounded sullen, but past caring. 'I'll give you my brother-in-law's address, which is near your offices and you can leave it with him.'

With that agreed, Grace got off the phone hurriedly, but I was angry. I did not believe that children's services had no place to store the scrapbook in case Angela contacted them in the future trying to find out about her son. I was sure that if I had been in her position I would have wanted to know my child was happy and healthy and would have been grateful for such a record of his young life. However, it was not to be, and within the week the book was back in my possession.

This whole scenario left a bitter taste. It seemed unbelievable that children's services were unwilling to file the book I had made up for Dale's biological mum. My reason for compiling it had been two-fold. The first, to keep a sympathetic link open, however tenuous, between Angela and Dale, and secondly, to be able to show Dale in the future that if he ever wanted to try and track down his birth parents, I would be open to helping him as much as I could. It seemed children's services preferred to sever all connections. I realised that I had never been given any information regarding contact for Dale with any of his birth family. Although I already knew that the adoptive parents of his half-brothers did not wish to have contact, I had always wondered why Dale's grandmother or aunt had never requested photos or information about Angela's little boy. It was a puzzle to me and it has not been clarified to date.

The big day arrived at last. June the 7th and the whole family was wide awake at the crack of dawn with excitement and in anticipation. I wanted everyone to look their best and I bathed both Cate and Dale before dressing them in the outfits David and I had chosen for the occasion. Cate, in particular, was very proud of her pretty dress. Jordan was taking a day off school to come with us and she looked absolutely gorgeous in her flowing gypsy skirt and aubergine top. Her long dark hair was shining and she looked every inch the proud big sister. I still could not believe that this day had come. After all the hostility and battling we had endured we were at last at the finishing line. All that it needed now was a signature from the Honourable Judge. The County Court building was as bustling as ever when we arrived but today there was a different feeling as we walked through the doors. All the unease of our earlier visits had vanished and now I felt light-hearted and unworried. Carla met us on our arrival; this would be her last duty as Dale's social worker and she seemed as excited as we were. She quickly briefed us on what to expect before an usher showed us into the large courtroom which, we were told, led to the judge's chambers where the actual signing of the adoption papers would take place.

At that moment the judge entered the room. He had a kindly, open face and I was surprised to see that instead of the customary black robes he wore a smart grey suit and was without the traditional wig. He must have noted my surprise and explained that when young children were part of the proceedings, he preferred them to see him as an ordinary person before the ceremony and formality of signing the adoption order. He joked with Cate and Dale and showed them a puppet; he told them it was his pet monkey who would be coming into chambers with us. By now both small children had picked up on the nervous anticipation that we were all feeling and they were bubbling over with excitement. David and I tried to calm them down but to no avail. Jordan was actually well accustomed to courts as she had an interest in pursuing a career in law and had already enjoyed a spell of work experience in this very place, but even she was beginning to get discomfited by the children's uncontrollable giggles in what was normally a very formal setting. I think the judge felt it was time to move on before things got completely out of control. With a big smile, he led us into his chambers and put on his robes. Then he showed Cate and Dale his wig before placing it on his head. They were enthralled and both wanted to try the wig on. The judge attempted to divert their attention from his hairpiece by pretending that the furry puppet creature was hiding from the children. Dale was laughing uproariously at the antics but Cate, to my total embarrassment, made a grab for the monkey and succeeded in ripping it from the judge's hand. She then jumped from her father's lap and began to race around the room shouting 'try and catch me' at the top of her voice. I turned a fiery shade of red and David tried his best to catch her as she ran past him for the third time. Dale thought it was all absolutely hysterical and tears of laughter were running down his cheeks whilst poor Jordan obviously wanted to hide her head in shame. Finally, we managed to stop Cate and wrestle the monkey puppet from her grasp. I handed it back to the judge just as Dale discovered the hole in the large desk, meant to accommodate computer leads. He was in the process of getting his small fist stuck in the orifice. The judge waited patiently while we eased it out. I then clamped my arms around Dale and David did the same with Cate.

When things eventually calmed down sufficiently, we moved on to the real reason we were in attendance, and the judge began to talk us through the signing of the adoption papers. He asked us about Dale's name, and whether we intended to change it, but we had already agreed that it would not be a good thing to do. Satisfied, and with everything finally in place, we put our signatures to the document. The judge endorsed it with his official seal and congratulated us. For an instant, it felt as though the world stopped. It was almost surreal. Unbelievably, after more than a year of fighting to make this little boy our own, we had actually done it. We were a complete family at last.

We filed into the courtroom again and Carla offered her congratulations all around. She agreed to take photos of us with the judge and we all posed together while she recorded the event. I was smiling for all I was worth. It was one of the happiest moments of my whole life. Everything we had gone through was worthwhile. Dale was safe and he was with us.

We were brought back to reality when Cate made a fast grab for the judge's wig and, putting it on her own head, ran off again at top speed. Mortified, I tried to stop her and eventually managed to retrieve it. The judge took it all in his stride, although I think he was probably glad to wave us all off from his courtroom that day.

Outside the court, I rang my mother.

'We did it! Hurrah.'

'Congratulations!' She shouted back from her classroom. 'Well done.'

We made more phone calls to other family members. Everyone was overjoyed for us. Finally, I rang Lindsay Parks, the solicitor who had helped to make it possible.

'Thank you so much for all your help.' I said.

'Not at all,' she replied. 'You all worked so hard to hold on to Dale – now go and enjoy him.'

'We intend to.' I told her gratefully.

Jubilant, Jordan and I decided to go shopping to celebrate while David took an absolutely exhausted Cate and Dale home. Their sprints around the courtroom seemed to have tired them out completely. When we returned home later that day, I was shattered too. I collapsed on the sofa and closed my eyes. My head was spinning and I felt overcome with emotion. I would not have to fight any more to hold on to Dale.

Epilogue – now

I am sitting at my computer desk writing this. The lights on the ceiling overhead are shaking. The children are meant to be playing quietly upstairs. It doesn't sound like a peaceful game of Barbie and Action Man to me. I can tell from the noise that Dale is leaping across Cate's bed, swinging on the upper posts as he does so. I can hear Cate's voice getting crosser as she tries to stop her five-year-old brother.

'Oh Dale! Stop it, stop it. I am going to tell Mammy'.

Now Dale is laughing, loud and full of fun. He is a real little boy. He loves aggravating Cate, getting a rise out of her, any way he can. He will deliberately take her doll and run to hide it in his own bedroom, well aware of the reaction he will get from Cate who hates him touching her things. I think they balance each other well. She is petite and dainty. He is big for his age and robust and sturdy. She is emotional and sensitive; he is less so but caring by nature. Cate will always cry if she is scared or hurts herself. Dale, on the other hand, is fearless and rarely gives in to tears. Cate enjoys dancing and singing while Dale loves any rough and tumble. He has recently begun playing football at a local school, and already the coaches are commenting on his ability, telling me how fast and strong he is. David, who is also very sporty, is keen to encourage Dale down the sporting route. He sees him as a future Olympic champion or maybe a Premier League footballer.

We are no longer foster carers. We resigned about a year after we adopted Dale. However, we remain great friends with both Dan and Jean, our support workers from the fostering agency. I am particularly proud that Jean asked David and me to provide her with our favourite piece of music to play at her wedding last year, knowing that we could not attend the event, which took place in the Caribbean.

We decided to stop fostering in order to have more time to enjoy our own children. Luckily, David's business was starting to establish itself and I also wanted to concentrate on a new challenge – writing. I thought *Dale's Tale* might be a good place to start.

Right now, the inspiration behind this story is laughing uproariously. The more Cate tells him to stop, the more he will aggravate and continue to annoy her. I hear Jordan shout across the landing, telling them to behave. I know from experience that they will both ignore her.

I can hear Dale racing toward his bedroom. He has snatched Cate's Barbie car from her. She is chasing after him in an attempt to snatch it back. I have to intervene now or else the car will be broken in the struggle.

This is a typical afternoon at our house. David will come home soon and hear the commotion from upstairs. He will probably shout quite loudly as he usually does, telling the children to stop. For a while they will obey and then it will start again until one of us separates them and sends them to their individual rooms for a while to calm down. Afterwards they will be contrite. They will say sorry and will want a cuddle from both David and me to reassure them that they are forgiven.

I think we are now a "normal" family – whatever that

means. Like any parents, we get cross with the children squabbling but we would not change anything. Sometimes David tells me I am too soft, that I give in too easily and let them get away with things they should not do. Other people seem to agree with his view. Maybe they are right. Maybe that is my nature. But I remember all too well the days when I thought we would not be fortunate enough to have Dale in our lives. I recall how much time and effort it took to get to where we are today. I can still count how many days I had to leave Cate and Dale with my mother so that I could go to court or attend meetings in an attempt to get my voice heard. Those recollections are still fresh in my mind and make me want to protect and spoil the children.

I feel lucky to be where we are today. If that makes me soft with them, then I am happy to be so. With Cate and Dale being so close in age, barely eighteen months between them, their behaviour can be wearing and challenging. I once read some research on optimal age gaps between children. It suggested that if the gap is less than twenty-four months, the older child may try to retain their baby status. I think to some extent that may well have been the case with Cate: she had to adjust to Dale's arrival when she had just turned two. On the other hand, Cate now seems to enjoy the status of being older than Dale. She regularly questions me about Dale getting bigger than her and I have to explain how he may indeed grow taller than her, but that she will always be older than him. She seems happy with that. Dale on the other hand gets annoyed when I say he is the baby in the family. He can't wait to be bigger and taller and laughs when I say that one day he may be bigger than his daddy.

When we were in the middle of the "crisis", I used to panic that all the effort I was forced to put into fighting to keep Dale might have had detrimental effects on all my children. There were days when I didn't think I could cope with the terrible anxiety and distress caused by the adoption team's reluctance to have us assessed. There were also numerous times when I wept bucket loads of tears at what I considered the unfairness to Dale, and I think at times like that, the children were definitely aware that something was wrong. Still, I look at us now and believe it was all worthwhile.

I don't imagine Dale or even Cate can really remember any of the anguish from the pre-adoption era and if there are tiny memories of those dark days, I think everyone would agree that it was a small sacrifice to make in order to be where we are now. We are whole. And Dale will grow up to know that he is loved and wanted by all of us. As a family, we will try to deal with the issues surrounding his adoption as sensibly and as sensitively as we can. There are sure to be some problems ahead for all of us and undoubtedly questions will arise and need to be handled. David and I worry sometimes about Dale's feelings when he is eventually old enough to understand what happened and becomes aware that he is not our "birth child". I hope that the very fact that Jordan is also not David's biological daughter will provide one common bond between them and help eliminate any underlying feelings Dale may harbour of being different. He will also understand, one day, how hard we fought to keep him and how difficult it must have been for his birth mother to let him go.

I would like to think that this story may help other families who find themselves in a similar dilemma. It is meant to be a story of hope and encouragement. The message is simple. Don't ever give up if you truly believe you have something worth fighting for.